FROM SHANTYTOWN TO TOWNSHIP

FROM
SHANTYTOWN
TO
TOWNSHIP

*An Economic Study of African Poverty and Rehousing
in a South African City*

Edited by

GAVIN MAASDORP

and

A. S. B. HUMPHREYS

Juta and Company Limited

CAPE TOWN   WYNBERG   JOHANNESBURG   DURBAN

© G. Maasdorp and A. S. B. Humphreys, 1975

January 1975

ISBN 0 7021 0569 4

✿ PRINTED IN THE REPUBLIC OF SOUTH AFRICA BY
THE RUSTICA PRESS (PTY.) LTD., WYNBERG, CAPE
297

Preface

This book had its origin in a survey conducted by the Durban Corporation in 1958. Soon after the completion of this survey, the assistance of the University of Natal's Department of Economics was enlisted, and this resulted in additional fieldwork in 1959. The results of these two projects were brought together in an unpublished manuscript, the main findings and conclusions of which were made available to the press. Thereafter, the Department's research unit continued to receive requests for information relating to the economic position of the African community in Durban, and thus in 1971 it was decided to incorporate an edited version of the original manuscript into an extended text which would compare the present economic position of Africans in Durban with the position in the earlier studies, taking into account the large-scale resettlement of Africans in new residential areas and the rapid economic growth experienced in South Africa during the 1960s.

The book is essentially a study of poverty and rehousing within the wider framework of rural–urban migration and urban growth in Africa, as well as within the peculiar economic, social and political structure of South Africa. The framework is outlined and related to the African community in the Durban metropolitan area in the Introduction.

Thereafter the book consists of two parts. In 1958–9 the great majority of Africans in Durban resided in Cato Manor, an area which consisted overwhelmingly of shacks. It was in this area that the earlier studies were undertaken. Their main features are summarized in Part I.

The remainder of the African population lived in the planned housing schemes of Chesterville, Lamont and Umlazi Glebe, while the new township of KwaMashu was receiving its first inhabitants who were being transferred from Cato Manor in terms of the Group Areas Act which enforces compulsory racial segregation in residential areas. The 1960s saw a period of rapid economic growth in the Durban metropolitan area and the completion of the resettlement programme involving the Cato Manor residents who were moved to KwaMashu and a further new township at Umlazi. The Bureau of Market Research at the University of South Africa conducted income and expenditure surveys among Durban Africans in 1964–5 and again in 1970–1, the publication of which has enabled us to chart changes in African incomes over a thirteen-year period.

iii

Part II deals with the resettlement of Africans in relation to continued rural–urban migration, discusses alternative approaches to the low-cost housing problem, describes the African townships as they exist today and examines changes in incomes and prices during this period. It includes a discussion of concepts of poverty as applied in South Africa, and analyses the reasons for the continued existence of large-scale poverty. The book is concluded with a chapter speculating on the future of the townships as a result of the establishment of KwaZulu, the 'homeland' for the Zulu people which, in terms of the stated goals of the policy of separate development, will ultimately achieve political independence.

The book, therefore, spans a fifteen-year period which was characterized by important economic, social and political events, affecting not only the African community of Durban but the entire country. The interaction of these economic, social and political forces has resulted in significant and perhaps permanent changes in political and economic relationships in Southern Africa.

The political unrest on the part of the Black peoples in South Africa gathered force during the 1950s and was climaxed by the incidents at Sharpeville and Langa in 1960 and the declaration of a state of emergency in both 1960 and 1961. Legislation was enacted which repressed political movements among the Black population groups and the consequent acts of sabotage, bannings and treason trials undermined confidence in the South African economy and gave rise to a recession in the early 1960s. However, the economy staged a remarkable recovery and maintained a high rate of growth during the remainder of the decade. But to some extent because of legislation preventing the optimum utilization of manpower, inflation was rampant throughout this period of recovery and led to a downturn in economic activity beginning in 1970.

Throughout the period, however, the job reservation laws (which exclude Blacks from certain occupations) were frequently suspended or overlooked and one result of economic growth has been that Coloureds, Indians and Africans have made significant strides up the occupational ladder. This has been accompanied by continued African migration from rural to urban areas—a movement which the government has attempted to counteract by following a policy of decentralization of industry to border areas and, more recently, to the African 'homelands', and by the passing of the Physical Planning Act of 1968 preventing further industrial expansion in declared (mainly urban) areas. This rural–urban migration has given rise to a continued programme of low-cost housing construction in the urban areas, but the housing problem, as viewed by officials, has still not been solved, as is evidenced by the growth of shack areas on the urban peripheries.

Concurrently, significant changes have occurred in the implementation of the policy of separate development. On the one hand, repressive legislation which further curtailed the rights of urban Africans was passed throughout the 1960s. On the other hand, the 1960s saw the creation of Territorial Authorities in various Bantustans or African 'homelands' and a more positive move towards the granting of political rights and ultimate political independence in these areas. As far as the African community of Durban is concerned, this resulted in the establishment in 1972 of a Legislative Assembly in KwaZulu (the new name for Zululand) as a first step in its path to independence. KwaZulu will ultimately include both of the larger African townships of Durban—a step which could lead to significant changes in their social and economic structure.

Throughout the text we have endeavoured to avoid the terms 'Native' and 'Bantu' when referring to the African people. These terms have acquired pejorative connotations and therefore are used only when quoting from official documents or citing the names of official organizations. Similarly we refer to the African, Coloured and Asian people collectively as 'Blacks' rather than as 'non-Whites' except when quoting from other sources.

It is impossible to conduct any study of this nature without the co-operation of official bodies, in this case the Durban Corporation and the government Department of Bantu Administration and Development. We are grateful to these bodies for permitting us to undertake fieldwork in the townships under their control. The township managers and various municipal officers, too numerous to mention individually, were always willing to assist us and to them we are greatly indebted.

The first-named editor wishes to thank those colleagues at the University of Natal and also, during a sabbatical term, at Queen Elizabeth House, Oxford, with whom the manuscript was discussed. At the University of Natal Harriet Sibisi (Institute for Social Research), Nesen Pillay (Economics), Colin Shum (African Studies) and Heinz Linhart (Mathematical Statistics) offered detailed comments on various portions of the manuscript, and Lawrence Schlemmer and Jane Ngobese (Institute for Social Research), Bruce Young (Geography) and Hilstan Watts (Sociology) made useful suggestions. He is particularly indebted to John Knight of the Oxford University Institute of Economics and Statistics for his incisive comments and suggestions on a draft outline of the book, and Heribert Adam of Simon Fraser University for his careful reading of the draft manuscript and his helpful criticisms, while Kenneth Kirkwood of St. Anthony's College, Oxford, also offered some valuable ideas. Peter Townsend of the University of Essex was instrumental in helping to clarify certain ideas relating to poverty. Tim Muil, African Affairs Correspondent of the *Natal Mercury*, provided many valuable insights into housing and migration in the metropolitan area.

The second-named editor wishes to thank in particular Mr

S. Bourquin, then Director of the Durban Corporation's Department of Bantu Administration, who was responsible for initiating the original study and for involving the university; Maurice Dhudla for his excellent supervision of the fieldworkers; and Merle Holden for undertaking the laborious task of converting the many tables in the original text into decimal currency.

The first draft of the manuscript was completed in April 1973. We wish to thank our fellow contributors for their co-operation in so promptly examining and commenting on the draft; this was of great help to us in preparing certain parts of the manuscript for submission to a series of multi-disciplinary seminars in August. Several useful suggestions emanated from these seminars and we wish to express our thanks to the participants.

We owe a special word of thanks to George Trotter, William Hudson Professor of Economics in the University of Natal, without whose encouragement this project would never have been completed; Philip Ellison who was indispensable in his editorial assistance; Susan Budd for her patience in typing the various drafts; and Don and Cynthia Sutherland and Hem Hurrypersad of the Department of Geography for preparing the maps.

We are grateful, too, to Professor F. E. Radel, sometime Director of the Bureau of Market Research, University of South Africa, for granting us permission to utilize the results of the Bureau's studies for comparative purposes.

It seems almost superfluous to add that responsibility for the opinions expressed and any errors contained in this book rest entirely with the contributors.

Durban and Pietermaritzburg   G.G.M.

October 1973   A.S.B.H.

The Contributors

JOHN R. BURROWS graduated at the University of Natal where he was Research Fellow in Economics from 1955 to 1961. He was subsequently government economist in Southern Rhodesia 1961–4; Senior Economist, Office of National Development and Planning, Zambian Government 1964–8; and Head, Agricultural Planning Unit, Zambian Ministry of Rural Development, 1968–9. Since 1969 he has been Staff Economist, International Bank for Reconstruction and Development, Washington, D.C. He is the author of *The Population and Labour Resources of Natal* (Pietermaritzburg, 1960) and contributed to Calvin B. Hoover (ed.), *Economic Systems of the Commonwealth* (Durham, N.C., 1962).

S. S. COOPPAN studied at the South African Native College, Fort Hare and obtained his doctorate at the University of Cape Town. After teaching and lecturing in Durban he held a British Council Scholarship in 1948–9 and lectured at Presidency College, Madras, from 1950 to 1953. He was Research Fellow in Economics at the University of Natal from 1954 to 1963 and was awarded a Brazilian Government Fellowship in 1961–2. He joined the Secretariat of the United Nations Economic Commission for Africa, Addis Ababa, in 1963 and is presently Chief, Education Unit, Manpower and Training Section, Human Resources Development Division. He was Senior Lecturer in Education at Macquarie University, Sydney in 1968–9. He has written numerous articles on Indian education in Natal.

PHILIP A. ELLISON graduated at the old Natal University College in 1932. After a lengthy career in education he became Research Assistant in Economics at the University of Natal in 1967. He is the co-author (with P. N. Pillay) of *The Indian Domestic Budget* (Durban, 1969), and has written various unpublished papers.

A. S. B. HUMPHREYS is a graduate of the universities of Witwatersrand and Cambridge. He was Assistant Economic Adviser in the Department of Commerce and Industries, Pretoria from 1939 to 1944 and Senior Economics Research Officer at the Leather Industries Research Institute, Rhodes University from 1944 to 1954. He was appointed Senior Research Fellow in the Department of Economics, University of Natal in 1954 and retired in 1966. He has contributed to *Experiment in Swaziland*, ed. J. F. Holleman (Cape Town, 1964) and various volumes of the Natal Regional Survey.

ZBIGNIEW A. KONCZACKI was born in Poland in 1917. He is a graduate of the universities of London and Natal. He was Research Fellow and Lecturer in Economics at the University of Natal from 1957 to 1962 and Associate Professor at the University of Alberta, Edmonton, from 1963 to 1967. In 1967 he assumed the Izaak Walton Killam Senior Research Fellowship at Dalhousie University, Nova Scotia, where he has been Professor of Economics since 1968. He has specialized in the problems of the less-developed countries with particular concentration on sub-Saharan Africa. He is the author of *Public Finance and Economic Development of Natal* 1893–1910 (Durham, N.C., 1967) and the co-editor of two forthcoming publications: *Pre-colonial Economic History of Africa South of the Sahara* and *An Economic History of Tropical Africa: Colonial Period* (London). He has contributed to *Problems of Economic Development*, eds. S. Chandrasekhar and C. W. Hultman (Boston, 1967). His numerous articles and papers have appeared in, *inter alia*, the *South African Journal of Economics* and the *Canadian Journal of African Studies*.

GAVIN MAASDORP is a graduate of the University of Natal where he became Research Fellow in Economics in 1964 and Senior Research Fellow in 1969. He studied at Boston University in 1967–8 on an Institute of International Education Scholarship and spent a sabbatical term in 1972 as Visitor at Queen Elizabeth House, Oxford. His publications include *A Natal Indian Community* (Durban, 1968) and contributions to *The Durban–Pietermaritzburg Region* (Durban, 2 vol., 1968 and 1969) and two forthcoming books: *Towards Comprehensive Development in KwaZulu*, ed. Lawrence Schlemmer (Durban) and *Contemporary Africa*, eds. C. G. Knight and J. L. Newman (Englewood Cliffs, N.J.). He has worked on research projects in Swaziland, Lesotho, the Transvaal and Natal.

Contents

List of Maps

INTRODUCTION

by
GAVIN MAASDORP

CHAPTER 1

The Study of an Urban African Community

In recent years increasing attention has been devoted, in the literature on less developed countries, to problems arising from rapid urbanization. In Africa it is not uncommon for the population of the larger towns and cities to grow at two or three times the national population growth rate, i.e. at 6–10 per cent per annum. The major causes of this rapid urbanization are the high rates of net rural–urban migration and natural increase.

RURAL–URBAN MIGRATION AND THE INFORMAL SECTOR

Economic development implies the structural transformation of the economy and is accompanied by the movement of population away from the agricultural sector to secondary and tertiary activities. This involves a shift of the population from rural to urban areas. In Africa this migration has been unusually rapid because of poverty in the rural areas and the labour demands of the modern sector of the economy focused on the cities which provide opportunities for wage employment.[1] The existence of substantial urban–rural wage differentials results in the cities exerting a magnetic pull on rural labour. Among other subsidiary factors stimulating migration are the attraction of the urban way of life and the existence, in the towns and cities, of better educational and health services.

Rural–urban migration may be seen as consisting of two elements, viz. first, temporary migration whereby individuals divide their time between wage employment in the towns and agricultural work in the rural areas, and second, a permanent drift to the towns which may involve entire families and which implies the emergence of a permanently urbanized community. Whilst a large amount of literature has accumulated on the subject there is as yet no satisfactory theory of migrant labour and the phenomenon is one which requires multi-disciplinary study.[2]

The migrant labour system has been criticized as being both socially and economically undesirable. Objections on social grounds stem largely from the separation of male migrants from their families. On economic grounds it has been argued that 'to the extent that many newly arrived migrants are likely to join the growing pool of unemployed and highly underemployed workers, and to the extent that an increasingly large proportion of these migrants represent the more educated segments of society whose productive potential is largely being dissipated, the process of continued rural–urban migration at

1

present levels can no longer be said to represent a desirable economic phenomenon'.[3]

Yet the economic efficiency of the system has been stressed by several writers who have analysed its impact on the supplying and receiving areas. Thus Miracle & Berry believe that the impact of migrant labour on economic development is likely to be complex and varied but challenge the assumption that the system is undesirable for economic reasons.[4] In his study of West Africa, Berg finds that migrant labour represents an efficient adaptation to the economic environment, benefiting both the labour exporting and recipient areas.[5] Bell attempts to show that migration represents economically rational behaviour. He argues that when the urban wage rate reaches a certain critical level in relation to agricultural output the migrant's individual contribution to family income is maximized by continuous wage employment; that income maximization requires that individuals undertake wage employment during those periods when marginal productivity in the rural areas is less than the wage rate; and that the higher the general wage level the more likely it is that continuous wage employment accompanied by family migration will be the income maximizing alternative.[6]

The phenomenon of rural–urban migration may be explained both in economic and sociological terms. The economic explanation is that migration occurs in response to income differentials, and the sociological that it reflects a preference for an urban way of life.[7] The aim of the migrant may well be to maximize not income but rather the utility of his family by considering material income as well as various social and political factors in his rural area.[8] In addition to expected income maximization, the degree of probability of obtaining a job has also been mentioned as a factor affecting the behaviour of the individual migrant.[9] Although migration is typically seen as more than merely an economic phenomenon, strong evidence in favour of an economic interpretation was found by Caldwell in his study of Ghana.[10]

Much of the economic literature on migration has centred on the disparity between rural and urban incomes.[11] Rural–urban income comparisons are difficult to make and must clearly be discussed in real terms.[12] The solution to the problem of income disparity between rural and urban areas involves policy matters relating to income distribution as well as political feasibility.[13] Among the measures which Todaro proposes in order to eliminate urban unemployment and disparities of expected incomes, and hence to reduce rural–urban migration, are an urban wage restraint policy, intensive agricultural and rural development policies, the limiting of population growth, and the development of domestic labour-intensive technological processes.[14]

An important point mentioned by Todaro is that at first the typical newly arrived migrant is either unemployed or else seeks casual or part-time employment in the urban traditional sector.[15] However, the recognition of an 'informal' sector in African cities is of recent origin[16] and the economic literature on migration has tended to be confined simply to the dichotomy between incomes in urban and rural areas and has neglected the existence of this informal sector. But this would not affect the broad conclusions of the analysis if, as the ILO mission to Kenya found, both formal and informal sector incomes exceed rural incomes.[17] For then migration clearly represents an improvement in income irrespective of whether work is found in the formal or informal sector and the rate of rural–urban migration can only be reduced if rural incomes can be increased in relation to formal and informal urban incomes.

A basic reason for the neglect of the informal sector is to be found in official census terminology, the definition of employment omitting the informal sector. This sector is, however, of considerable importance in African cities. In Kenya it provided 28–33 per cent of African urban employment in 1969—a figure which was considered low when compared with other African countries.[18] And in Ghana Hart shows that in a slum district of Accra some 60 per cent of the working-age population were not touched by wage employment.[19] But in addition to the wage sector a wide range of income opportunities was open to them; 'denied success by the formal opportunity structure, these members of the urban sub-proletariat seek informal means of increasing their incomes'.[20] Examples of such activities are those of self-employed artisans (e.g. shoemakers, tailors, carpenters, builders and masons), beer brewers and liquor distillers and sellers, pirate taxi operators, petty traders, hawkers, caterers, cooks, barbers, witch-doctors and moneylenders. The illegal activities of usurers, pawn-brokers, drug-pushers, prostitutes, smugglers, confidence tricksters, gamblers and petty thieves are included in the informal sector. Petty capitalism is frequently a supplement to wage employment. Those engaged in such activities are not enumerated under 'establishments' and are therefore not classified as 'economically active'.

There are many conceptual difficulties in defining unemployment in African urban areas, and the question that arises is: how many are truly unemployed? Unorganized workers, e.g. shoeshine boys, are usually regarded as 'underemployed' because their activities are only marginally productive, while those persons lacking formal employment are classified as 'unemployed'. Many of the concepts used in censuses and statistical surveys are, however, inapplicable in less developed countries. Hart argues that value-laden Western concepts are applied indiscriminately to African conditions—the term 'underemployed' is based on an assumption about the level of productivity, and the only truly 'unemployed' are 'those who will not accept income opportunities open to them for which they are qualified . . .'.[21] This is supported by the ILO mission, which produced evidence showing that 'the bulk of employment in the informal sector, far from being only marginally productive, is economically efficient and profit–making ... offering virtually the full range of basic skills needed to provide goods and services for a large though often poor section of the population'.[22]

The high level of officially–defined unemployment in most African cities resulting from migration flows outstripping the creation of wage employment opportunities is regarded as a major economic, social and political problem. Rural migrants face considerable problems in adjusting to urban life,[23] but these problems are compounded by the shortage of jobs, which leads to the inefficient use of manpower, poverty (in the form of inadequate household incomes), socially undesirable behaviour (crime and prostitution) and political unrest (due to the creation of frustration and discontent). But if cognizance is taken of the informal sector the question becomes not one of how to create more wage employment but rather one of whether 'we want to shift the emphasis of income opportunities in the direction of formal employment for its own sake or only to reduce participation in socially disapproved informal activities and in those informal occupations whose marginal productivity is too low'.[24]

Another important consequence of rural–urban migration is the emergence of uncontrolled shack settlements on the urban periphery. This is common in African towns; for example, in Lusaka squatters comprise one-half of the population.[25] These settlements may give rise to overcrowding and concomitant social and health problems, and their elimination places a strain on the financial resources of the local authorities, who find it difficult to provide an adequate standard of urban services, e.g. streets, electricity, piped water, sanitation, health services, etc., in such areas. The absence of such services is often exacerbated by the unsympathetic view of squatter settlements which is adopted by officials and the general public, and the constant harassment of the squatters may lead to political discontent. Low–cost housing programmes financed by the central government thus tend to be allocated a high priority in less developed countries in order to eliminate shack areas and hence alleviate political and social unrest, and scarce resources have to be diverted to such projects.

In this connection the recognition of the informal sector may introduce important modifications in thinking. The ILO mission to Kenya, for example, felt that the too stringent imposition of modern standards of design, building specifications and materials was inapplicable in an African context.[26] Provided no threat to public health was posed, these standards could be relaxed; many shack dwellings required only minor expenditure and modification to become satisfactory, and expenditure on large low–cost housing projects could be channelled into informal sector schemes with more flexible standards which would provide many more units of housing.

The importance of rural–urban migration is seen throughout this study of the economic position of an urban African community, while the informal sector is touched on at several points. An attempt at the provision of intermediate-standard housing in Durban is described later in this chapter, while chapter 3 provides a detailed discussion of sources of supplementary income, i.e. income derived mainly from informal activities. The scope for informal sector housing is again mentioned in chapters 4 and 7.

THE URBANIZATION OF AFRICANS IN SOUTH AFRICA

Urbanization in South Africa received its impetus from the development of the mining industry from 1870 onwards and the growth of secondary industry following the First World War. Industrial growth was stimulated particularly by the adoption of a policy of tariff protection for local industries in 1925 and later by the Second World War. South Africa exhibits the greatest degree of urbanization of any major country in Africa,[27] the urban population having increased as a proportion of the total from 23,6 per cent in 1904 to 39,3 per cent in 1946 and 48,0 per cent in 1970.[28]

Africans are the least urbanized of the four race groups in South Africa, but show the most rapid rate of urbanization. The proportion of Africans who are urbanized has trebled in this century, having risen from 10,4 per cent in 1904 to 33,1 per cent in 1970. During this period the comparative respective percentages for Whites were 53,6 and 86,9, for Coloureds 49,2 and 74,0, and for Asians 36,5 and 86,9.

The province of Natal is less urbanized than the country as a whole. This is largely due to the fact that there are proportionately more Africans in Natal—75,7 per cent (or 3 213 000 of the total population of 4 246 000 in 1970) than in South Africa (70 per cent)—and that only 25,2 per cent of Natal Africans are urbanized. Despite the fact

Table 1.1

URBAN AFRICAN POPULATION, NATAL, 1904–70

Census year	Total Urban Population ('000)		Africans as % of total
	African	All races	
1904	36	123	29,2
1911	39	173	22,5
1921	82	267	30,7
1936	143	425	33,6
1946	218	595	36,6
1951	288	771	37,4
1960	421	1 081	38,8
1970	811	1 713	47,3

Sources: Department of Statistics, Pretoria, *1965 Statistical Year Book*, and 1970 Population Census, Report 02–05–01.

that the proportion of urbanized Africans in Natal has increased over sixfold since 1904 (when it was 4 per cent), the figure is low compared with the 90 per cent of Whites and Coloureds and 84,7 per cent of Asians in Natal who are urbanized.

Table 1:1 reveals that almost one-half of the urban population of Natal in 1970 was African. However, the figures are not strictly comparable as allowance must be made for changes in the census definition of urban areas over time. Moreover, the census figures in respect of Africans are notoriously unreliable, in regard both to absolute numbers and geographic distribution, reflecting the general difficulties of census-taking in Africa. According to Sadie the African population was underenumerated by 5,2 per cent in 1960; the deficiency occurred mainly in the most mobile labour force age group (15–39 years) and is attributed to the migrant labour system.[29]

LEGISLATION AND THE URBAN AFRICAN

Industrial development in South Africa created a growing demand for African labour and this resulted in the establishment of a permanent African population in the urban areas. However, the growth of the urban African population has been controlled by legislation which has also affected employment and housing.

In order to control the rural–urban migration of Africans, influx control regulations were promulgated in terms of the Natives (Urban Areas) Act No. 21 of 1923 (amended by Acts Nos. 25 of 1930 and 46 of 1937 and later replaced by the Natives (Urban Areas) Consolidation Act No. 25 of 1945). In addition to controlling the migration of Africans to urban areas, this Act also sought to control African employment in urban areas, the establishment of townships and the administration of urban African affairs.[30] The permanent settlement, on any significant scale, of African families in urban areas was prevented, while the supply of and demand for African labour was controlled by the establishment of a network of labour bureaux. (The effects of these bureaux will be examined in chapter 6.)

The Fagan Report of 1948 was critical of the perpetuation of the migrant labour system and advocated a policy of encouraging the establishment of stable family units in urban areas.[31] However, the National Party government was elected in 1948 and subsequently embarked upon a policy of racial segregation which involved the passing of legislation affecting almost every aspect of the lives of urban African and other Black communities. Thus the provisions of the renamed Bantu (Urban Areas) Consolidation Act No. 54 of 1952 and allied laws were broadened by the Bantu Laws Amendment Acts No. 76 of 1963 and No. 19 of 1970.[32]

Since 1923 successive Acts have made it more difficult for Africans to qualify for residence in urban areas. In terms of the 1923 Act Africans had to report to a registering officer within 48 hours of arrival in an urban area. Such registration could not be refused if accommodation was available, but workers were required to obtain contracts of service. Female travel was not restricted and thus families could remain together. This was, however, soon changed, the 1930 amendment allowing local authorities to prohibit female entry and the 1937 amendment imposing further restrictions. The 1952 Act prevented Africans from staying in urban areas for more than 72 hours unless they had been born and were permanently resident there, or had worked continuously for one employer for ten years, or had been in the area for at least fifteen years.

The urban areas have always been regarded as part of 'White' South Africa. Africans in these areas have been considered temporary sojourners, their legitimate home being the Reserves (now officially referred to as homelands). Thus the Native Land Act No. 27 of 1913 had demarcated areas for the sole occupation of Africans outside of which they were not permitted to acquire land. As a consequence Africans have never been allowed to own property in Durban.

However, it is the Group Areas Act No. 41 of 1950[33] which has had the greatest effect on the housing of Africans—and indeed of all communities—in Durban.[34] The aim of the Group Areas Act is to set aside areas each to be occupied exclusively by one race group. In the urban areas this involves the creation of separate residential areas for each race group. The Group Areas Board first began investigating proposals for the establishment of Group Areas in Durban in 1955.

THE AFRICAN COMMUNITY OF DURBAN

The position with regard to African population growth and housing in South African cities can be understood only in the context of the migrant labour system and the elaborate legal framework affecting urban Africans. But before discussing the African community of Durban, it is necessary to say a brief word about the metropolitan area itself.

THE DURBAN METROPOLITAN AREA

In 1824 a small British settlement was established at the Bay of Natal. The township of Durban was laid out in 1835 and was accorded borough (or municipal) status in 1854. Today Durban is the central city of the second largest metropolitan area in South Africa. The 1970 census gave the population of the Durban metropolitan area (DMA) as 1 035 000; it is multiracial in composition, with 395 000 Africans, 330 000 Indians, 264 000 Whites and 45 000 Coloureds. The DMA stretches along the coast south of Durban as far as Umbogintwini, inland as far as Kloof and northwards to include KwaMashu (Map 1).

The economy of the DMA is reasonably diversified. The port of Durban is the largest on the African continent in terms of cargo

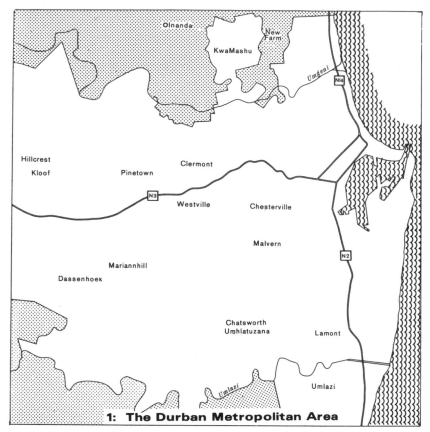

1: The Durban Metropolitan Area

handled, and serves a rich hinterland which includes the Pretoria–Witwatersrand–Vereeniging industrial region (the largest in the country). There has been a rapid growth of manufacturing industry in the DMA since 1925, and especially since the great depression of the early 1930s. Thus the DMA today accounts for some 12 per cent of the net value of output in the manufacturing and construction industries in South Africa. Manufacturing industry in the DMA is based on chemicals and petroleum products, food, clothing and textiles, metal products, paper and printing, rubber products and various other items. In addition, a wide range of commercial and other service activities is found in the area, and Durban itself is South Africa's major tourist and vacation centre.

AFRICAN POPULATION GROWTH

Africans have resided in Durban since its establishment. The first municipal census held in 1862 showed that of the population of 4 300 some 1 600 were Africans.[35]

According to the municipal census held in 1911, there were 19 000 Africans in Durban, constituting 21 per cent of the city's population.

In 1932 the city area was extended from 12 to 70 square miles by the inclusion of various peri-urban areas (known as the 'added areas'). This resulted in a substantial increase in the municipal population, the pre-incorporation total of 126 000 rising by 74 per cent to 218 000. Incorporation had the effect of altering the racial composition of the city's population; the number of Indians almost trebled while the estimated African population rose by almost one-half, from 43 800 to 64 600. In 1946 Africans numbered 111 000 (30,4 per cent of the population) and in 1960, 182 000 (32,6 per cent). By 1970, owing to large-scale resettlement outside the municipal area, the number had been reduced to 99 500 (22,5 per cent).

However, in any urban agglomeration data on the metropolitan population are more important than those relating only to the central city. Table 1:2 portrays the growth of the African population of the DMA to 1970.

Table 1.2

AFRICAN POPULATION, DURBAN METROPOLITAN AREA, 1921–1970

Census year	African Population	
	No.	% of total
1921	46 000	27,2
1936	71 000	26,6
1946	114 000	30,6
1951	162 000	32,5
1960	222 000	32,6
1970	395 000	38,2

Sources: John R. Burrows, *The Population and Labour Resources of Natal*, 1959, pp. 24–5; 1960 Population Census, Vol. 1, Geographical Distribution of the Population, Table 7; 1970 Population Census, Report 02–05–01.

The figures in this table should be treated with some caution since the extent of underenumeration in metropolitan areas such as Durban is perhaps greater than in the rural areas. It is generally thought that large numbers of people who are illegally residing in the urban areas avoid being enumerated. Moreover, it is still customary for many African migrants to return to the Reserves for the census in order to be recorded as members of their families. In 1960 an additional complicating factor was that the census was conducted at a time of deep political unrest following the incidents at Sharpeville and Langa earlier in that year. The prevalent mood on the part of township dwellers was one of antagonism and non-cooperation towards the authorities, and the census figures were probably seriously underestimated. Estimates of underenumeration of Africans in certain South African cities in 1970 vary from 17 to 50 per cent.[36]

But the figures do show that, despite the adoption of measures to control rural–urban migration described below, Africans have increased as a proportion of the total population. Migration has continued unabated, and a study undertaken in the late 1950s showed that only 1,7 per cent of the male African labour force of the city was originally from the Durban magisterial district.[37] Even if the Umlazi, Ndwedwe, Inanda and Pinetown districts which adjoin Durban were taken into consideration, this proportion was increased to only 21,5 per cent. The remainder of the male labour force was drawn from districts throughout Natal and, to a lesser extent, the Transkei.

A change in the racial composition of the labour force is one of the most important features of industrial growth in the DMA. During the war permanent changes occurred in the structure of the industrial labour force. African employment in manufacturing industry rose from 10 900 in 1934–5 to 28 900 in 1944–5—a mean annual rate of increase of over 10 per cent, which was the highest of all the race groups. Africans increased from 43 per cent of the manufacturing labour force in 1939–40 to 50 per cent in 1944–5.[38]

Concurrent with this period of rapid industrial expansion was a rapid flow of Africans to the city. The extent to which officialdom was unaware of the precise magnitude of this flow is shown by municipal population estimates. The estimated African population of the Durban municipal area increased from 64 700 in 1938 to 73 300 in 1943, yet the 1946 census revealed a population of 104 600, indicating a serious underestimate in the municipal figures.

The flow of Africans to Durban continued in the post-war years, and the municipal estimates jumped sharply from 109 500 in 1949 to 127 500 in 1950. This was a result of a count of the inhabitants of shack housing, the existence of which made it very difficult to estimate the population with any degree of accuracy. However, such counts brought home to the municipal authorities the true population picture, which was not revealed in official censuses. Thus whereas the 1951 census figure for the Durban African population was 132 800, the municipal estimate was 150 000–160 000.

Further evidence of the growth of the African population is found by examining data relating to the total number of males in registered employment in Durban on 31 July each year. This shows that the number increased from some 91 600 in 1949 to 115 400 in 1955. During the second half of the 1950s there was little increase in registered employment and by 1959 the figure had reached only 120 000.

An important demographic feature of the African population of the DMA has been a marked decline in the sex ratio. According to the 1921 census there were 6,6 males for every female; this figure declined to 3,4 in 1936, 2,1 in 1951, 1,5 in 1960 and 1,2 in 1970. This levelling off in the sex ratio is indicative of a more stable and mature urban population with a greater degree of family life and a declining relative importance of migrant labour.

HOUSING

The need for a residential area for Africans in Durban was felt as early as 1863. However, despite the recommendation in the same year that land should be set aside for this purpose, the selection of a site in 1873 and further demands for an African residential area (or'location') in 1886 and 1889, it was only after the turn of the century that municipal accommodation was provided. Municipal barracks for dockworkers were built at the Point in 1903 and were followed by the Depot Road Location (which subsequently developed into the Somtseu Road Location) in 1913. These projects provided for the accommodation of male migrant workers, and it was not until the establishment of Baumannville in 1915–16 that family cottages were built.[39] The situation of the various African residential areas mentioned in this study is depicted in Map 2.

In the towns of colonial Africa residential segregation of the races often started spontaneously or as a result of the fear of epidemics and disease. Moreover, there were also fundamental social and cultural differences.[40] Durban was no exception; segregation of Africans arose from a desire on the part of the colonists to reduce illegal liquor traffic, theft, assault and the risk of fire, to protect health standards and to maintain property values.[41] Once it began segregation in colonial Africa was invariably enforced by law, and in South Africa it has been a cornerstone of the policy of successive governments.

Baumannville represented the first real attempt at eliminating the undesirable conditions in which the African community was living. Africans were 'housed haphazardly in employers' backyards, in washhouses, store-rooms or private compounds'.[42] The haphazard and largely uncontrolled housing of Africans was typical of South African towns prior to 1923, when the Natives (Urban Areas) Act was promulgated. This Act vested local authorities with the sole right of, and responsibility for, providing for the accommodation of Africans in segregated areas. All Africans other than those exempted under the Act, or employed in bona fide domestic service in urban areas, were obliged to take up their residence in a 'location', village or hostel, or in premises specially licensed by the local authority for the accommodation of Africans.

Finance was a major problem confronting the local authorities in the provision of housing. The position was alleviated by the Native Beer Act of 1908 which empowered local authorities to utilize the profits from their monopoly sales of 'kaffir beer' for the erection of houses, schools, hospitals and other facilities for Africans. In Durban in 1923 the Native Revenue Account derived its income from beer profits, licence fees for certain occupations, e.g. caterers, ricksha pullers and 'togt' labourers,[43] and rent from municipal housing. But the account showed an overdraft of R60 000 and the Central Housing Board had rejected a loan application for R200 000 owing to lack of

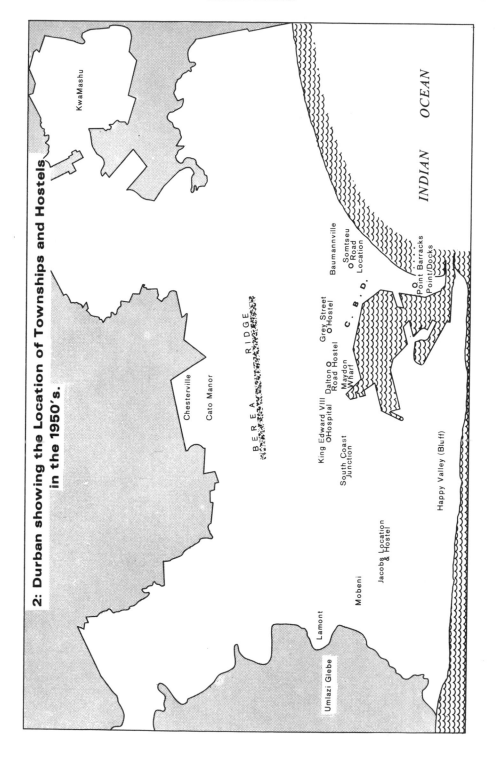

2: Durban showing the Location of Townships and Hostels in the 1950's.

funds.[44] This was at a time when the expansion of port activities, the building of the graving dock and grain elevators and the initiation of municipal water and housing schemes were creating an increased demand for African labour.

During the period 1923–37 the authorities were concerned chiefly with housing migrant workers in hostels and compounds. In 1923, 46 000 Africans were housed in such accommodation in Durban. Although a class of permanent town dwellers had emerged, the African population was largely a floating one due to the proximity of the Reserves, and there was little demand for family housing prior to the enlargement of the municipal area in 1932 by the incorporation of the 'added areas'. However, in 1930 the Durban Corporation had purchased 3 000 acres of Clairwood Estate for conversion into a residential area for Africans. In 1933–4, as a consequence of the considerable influx of Africans into Durban following the recovery in economic activity after the depression of 1929–33, the first houses of the Lamontville Location (later known simply as Lamont) were built on Clairwood Estate. Baumannville was completed in 1934.

In 1937 the Natives (Urban Areas) Act became operative over the whole of the Durban municipal area. As a consequence, the Durban Corporation was compelled to augment available municipal housing accommodation for Africans resident within its boundaries, and therefore embarked on a large housing programme. Thus 400 additional cottages were built at Lamont in 1937 and extensions were made to the Somtseu Road Location. Hostel accommodation for African women was provided at Grey Street in 1936 and Jacobs in 1939, while men's hostels were built at Dalton Road in 1934, the Point (Bell Street and Plymouth Road) also in 1934, Somtseu Road in 1938 and Jacobs in 1939.

Such a programme was urgently needed in order to overcome the problems raised by the incorporation of the 'added areas'. These areas were characterized by the type of uncontrolled growth commonly found on the periphery of African cities. The dwellings were poorly constructed, overcrowded and insanitary, and conditions did not fulfil municipal housing and health standards. By 1936 it was clear that, due to rapid urbanization, the provision of adequate housing for Africans would present Durban with a serious problem. The housing programme in the late 1930s and the general system of municipal African administration in Durban were regarded at the time as models to be followed by other local authorities—in fact, the Durban system of administration had formed the basis for the Natives (Urban Areas) Act of 1923.

It was after the outbreak of the war in 1939 that the most serious shortage of African housing developed. There was a large and rapid influx of population into Durban due to growing pressure on the land and poverty in the Reserves and the labour needs of the city's expanding industries and increased commercial and shipping activities which were stimulated by the war. In addition, the wartime restrictions on building activities precluded the construction of large-scale housing schemes for all sections of the population. The result was increased congestion in existing housing and the appearance of unauthorized 'shanty towns' and illegal squatters' camps and shack areas—conditions which were common to all South African cities at the time. The new arrivals tended to congregate in the Cato Manor area where there had been a scattering of isolated shacks since 1928.

The Smuts government (1939–48) has often been criticized for its failure to cater for the huge urban drift of Africans. However, building materials were in scarce supply and wartime restrictions had to be strictly implemented. It is an often overlooked fact that despite these difficulties 900 houses were built at Blackhurst Estate (later renamed Chesterville) between 1940 and 1945. But this fell far short of the demand for housing and the deficiency was not made good in the immediate post-war years despite the completion of Chesterville in 1946 and an extension at Lamont between 1946 and 1950.

Since much of this study is concerned with Cato Manor, the growth of this area deserves special attention. Cato Manor (Map 3) consists of broken and undulating land originally owned by Whites but later sold to Indians.[45] Before the war it was one of the main banana-producing areas of Natal. During the 1930s there was a steady growth of shacks in the Blackhurst and Booth Road areas of Cato Manor, and by 1939 there were 500 shacks. During and after the war migrants from the rural areas tended to concentrate in Cato Manor. This area, lying between the southern spur of the Berea Ridge and Chesterville is roughly within three kilometres of the old industrial area of central Durban and within five kilometres of the industrial areas of Mobeni and Jacobs.

Africans are not allowed to own land in the urban areas and, in the absence of sufficient municipal and employer-provided accommodation, were obliged to rent sites from Indian landowners in the hilly market gardening areas of Cato Manor. In many cases the leasing of land for shacks was more profitable than market gardening, and a class of slum landlords emerged. Africans were able to rent sites cheaply upon which they could construct home-made shelters. Thus clusters of wood and iron shacks and lean-to's sprang up in areas beyond the reach of municipal water and sanitary services. About one-half of Durban's African population was illegally housed in such shack areas. Overcrowding was rife, and a 1943–4 housing survey showed that over one-half of all Africans outside the municipal locations were living in overcrowded conditions.

Thus the geographic proximity of Cato Manor to the city and the profitability of renting plots for shack-building resulted in the rapid growth of a squatters' camp at Cato Manor, where the population increased from 2 500 persons in 1936 to more than 17 000 in 1943.

In the Booth Road area alone there were 5 000 Africans residing in 700 shanties in 1943. By the following year these figures had risen to 17 000 and 3 000 respectively, and in 1948 an estimated 27 000 Africans lived in this area.

The *Durban Housing Survey* estimated that in 1950 there were 8 000 African shack dwellings in Durban housing some 67 500 persons. In Cato Manor alone some 6 000 shacks contained a population of 45 000–50 000, while there were 1 000 shacks in the South Coast Junction area, 700 at Happy Valley on the Bluff and 300 at Umhlatuzana.[46]

It was not only Africans who were shack dwellers; large numbers of Indians also migrated to Durban and lived in similar conditions. For some years the authorities clearly underestimated the population in these areas. For example, a 1946 survey found 5 500 African families living in shacks, mainly in Cato Manor; the population of 30 000 was estimated on the assumption of some five persons per shack. By 1949 the number of shacks in Durban had increased to 7 200 and by 1950 to 8 560 housing an estimated 42 800 Africans and Indians. But a 1951 municipal study revealed an average of 8,8 persons per shack and the 9 860 shacks were therefore estimated to house 86 800 persons. In 1952 there were 10 100 shacks accommodating an estimated 89 000 persons of whom Africans probably numbered at least 70 000. Throughout its existence the shack area of Cato Manor was essentially African.

The shack areas provided considerable scope for the existence of an informal sector. With the steady flow of migrants requiring shelter, African building contractors made their appearance and erected shacks for the new arrivals. Others operated as unlicensed traders (mainly fresh produce and general dealers), or as hawkers or pedlars of meat and offal at the roadside; in some areas unlicensed 'buying clubs' functioned as shops. Some elderly women took in washing, and in areas with no fresh-water supplies, water for drinking and cooking was purchased from African carriers. Backyard motor mechanics, painters and other self-employed artisans were also found.

The lack of fresh water and sanitation meant that the shack areas constituted a health hazard to the city. There were periodic outbreaks of typhoid fever, and gastro-enteritis and amoebic dysentery were rife. Because of topographical features and the absence of suitable access roads, municipal sanitary services were available only at certain central points. Prior to 1951 the City Council lacked the legal machinery to prevent shack-building and the power to demolish illegally erected structures. Attempts by the Corporation to compel landowners to provide basic sanitation were held up by protracted litigation; moreover, many landlords would rather have evicted their tenants than provide these services. However, in 1951 the City Council acquired the authority (in terms of Ordinance 21 of 1949) to demolish shacks which were vacant, in the process of erection or occupied if alternative accommodation was available.

The already serious African housing position was aggravated by the 'Durban riots' of January 1949. These disturbances, involving violence between Indians and Africans, resulted in the destruction of property and rendered some families homeless. The riots were centred on Cato Manor; some Indian landlords lost control of the use of their land and the number of African shacks increased considerably. By 1950, therefore, the City Council faced a grave problem so far as the housing of the African community was concerned.

During the war the Council had established a special committee to consider post-war housing requirements. This committee found that 2 300 houses would be needed for Africans in the first five years after the war and a further 1 500 houses during the second five years. A problem was posed by the limited availability of land suitable for housing and convenient to the main transport routes. However, the Umlazi Mission Reserve some 16–19 kilometres south of the city centre suggested itself as a suitable area, and the City Council, with the support of the Natal Provincial Administration, made representations to the government to acquire all or part of the Reserve. This was refused, and in 1949 the new National Party government announced its own plans to urbanize the area completely independently of the responsibility of the City Council for housing its African community.

The City Council experienced further difficulties which delayed the implementation of a large-scale housing programme. After devaluation in 1949 the Treasury instructed that capital expenditure be cut, and thus in 1949–50 approved housing schemes were either curtailed or abandoned. In 1950 the City Council resolved to acquire part of Cato Manor for a permanent housing scheme; this was approved by the Administrator of Natal in 1951 but was immediately rejected by the government until such time as a permanent zoning scheme under the Group Areas Act had been approved.

Residential segregation by race in South African cities was perhaps more complete in Durban than anywhere else; indeed, the appearance of inter-racial neighbourhoods during the war by the so-called 'Indian penetration' led to vehement protests and the passing of legislation (in 1943 and 1946) to control this movement. But following the advent to power of the National Party in 1948, racial segregation was given an ideological basis ('apartheid'). The Group Areas Act was the instrument by which strict residential segregation of all races was to be enforced.

In the meantime, pending the Group Areas zoning, attempts were made to provide accommodation in the main urban areas through the establishment of controlled 'emergency camps' where Africans were permitted to erect temporary structures for which basic services were provided by municipal authorities until suitable permanent accommodation could be built elsewhere.[47] Thus, after protracted negotiations, the Durban Corporation acquired a total of 558 acres (226 ha) of land at Cato Manor in 1952 for the purposes of establishing an 'Emergency Camp'.

This was essentially an attempt at providing the type of informal housing discussed earlier in this chapter. The basic services provided by the Corporation comprised roads, stormwater drainage, street lights and ablution blocks with toilets and washing facilities. Terraced sites were laid out on which families could erect shacks under supervision. Sites were also made available for schools, churches, community halls, sports grounds, crèches, shops and a transit camp which finally consisted of 183 rooms. To assist residents in the building of their shacks, loans of up to R40 were made available, repayable (with an economic charge for interest) at the rate of R1 per month.

The Emergency Camp, however, proved totally inadequate to cope with the rapidly growing population of Cato Manor. The geography and topography of the countryside surrounding the Emergency Camp precluded any significant expansion of the camp area with the result that uncontrolled shack areas, lacking even the most rudimentary community services, continued to grow on the fringes of the camp and, on a smaller scale, in other isolated localities in and around Durban.

The S. J. Smith Hostel for single males was built in 1950 and the Umlazi Glebeland area, adjoining Lamont, was established as a permanent African housing area in the same year. But further expansion of the Chesterville housing scheme (which adjoined Cato Manor) to accommodate this growing shack population was not undertaken because, in terms of government policy, the Cato Manor area was earmarked for occupation by Whites under the Group Areas Act.[48] Instead, an area of 2 261 acres (915 ha) of sugar-cane estates, originally owned by Natal Estates Limited, was acquired in 1953 by the Durban Corporation at Duff's Road, 18 kilometres north of Durban, for the establishment of an extensive African housing scheme to be known as KwaMashu.[49]

The Group Areas Act, in fact, delayed the solution of the African housing problem in Durban by several years. It was not until 1956 that KwaMashu was proclaimed a municipal housing scheme and building could commence.

As this new accommodation became available, shack households with monthly incomes amounting to R30 or more were transferred to the new accommodation and their shacks were demolished. In view, however, of the relatively limited number of shack households which were in receipt of declared monthly incomes of R30 or more, the building programme at KwaMashu threatened, at one stage, to outstrip the number of prospective occupants selected on this basis. In consequence, the qualifying income level was successively reduced from R30 to R24 and finally to R22 per month without, however, any equivalent reduction in the economic rentals charged for the new accommodation. These higher rentals, the increased transport costs involved because of the greater distance between KwaMashu and places of employment in Durban, and opposition encountered from various vested interests in the shack areas, led to considerable resistance to this transfer by the shack dwellers and in 1959 there were serious clashes with the police.

The resettlement programme and subsequent housing developments will be discussed in chapter 4.

POVERTY STUDIES

In African cities the most important difficulty associated with housing programmes is the 'inability of most residents to pay rent on even the lowest cost homes'.[50] In Durban, too, the main problem faced by the local authority in effecting the transfer of those living in temporary emergency camps and illegal shack areas to permanent housing schemes was to provide improved accommodation which would be within the limited means of the people to be rehoused.

Mass housing is usually provided on both an economic and sub-economic basis. Although the new accommodation represents a substantial improvement on the old from the point of view of modern standards, the higher rentals involved exacerbate the already parlous economic position of the families. This has two important consequences. Either the families default in rent payments, thereby providing administrative difficulties for the housing authority, or they are forced to sacrifice food and other essentials in order to meet rental commitments, thereby endangering the workers' health and productivity and the welfare of their families. They may also be forced to restrict their participation in social life and withdraw from their family network.[51] An important focus of this work, therefore, is on the family budgets of the African community of Durban.

The seminal work in the field of family budget studies is that of Prais & Houthakker.[52] Theirs is an econometric study directed mainly at the analysis of consumers' behaviour. It is, in fact, an expenditure study in which Engel curves are applied to various items of consumer expenditure. In contrast, this work is concerned with poverty, and therefore the income as well as the expenditure side is examined.

Poverty studies have a long history, dating back to the pioneering works of Booth and Rowntree in England.[53] In South Africa the measure commonly used for assessing the level of poverty in a community is the 'Poverty Datum Line' (PDL) which was developed by Batson.[54] This is a modification of Bowley's method[55] which in turn was an improvement on that of Rowntree.

The PDL estimates the lowest possible amount on which the average family can live under humanly decent conditions in the short run. In other words, it measures the theoretical minimum cost of living of a household. It consists of two parts, viz. the Primary and the Secondary

PDL. The *Primary PDL* consists of food, clothing, cleansing materials, and fuel and lighting. The calculation takes into account the varying needs of persons of different age and sex in the household. The costs of food and clothing for each individual are totalled, and to this total is added the household component for cleansing materials and fuel and lighting, i.e. the costs of running a household irrespective of its size. The *Secondary PDL* is obtained by adding to the primary figure the cost of accommodation, transport of workers to and from work, and direct taxation.

The PDL excludes many items on which income is normally expended. This is clearly illustrated in a well-known passage by Batson who writes: It 'allows only for the indispensable minimum quantities of food, clothing, fuel, lighting, cleaning, housing and transport to and from work. It allows nothing for amusements, sports, hobbies, education, medicine, medical or dental care, holidays, newspapers, stationery, tobacco, sweets, gifts or pocket-money or for comforts or luxuries of any kind or for replacement of household equipment and furniture or for hire-purchase or insurance or saving. It is clear that the Poverty Datum Line does not indicate a "human" standard of living. It merely fulfils its purpose of stating the barest minimum expenditure by which subsistence, health and decency can theoretically be achieved under Western conditions taking only "short-run" considerations into account.'[56]

A 'human' standard of living can be approached only when household income exceeds the Secondary PDL. The margin of excess required is usually regarded as 50 per cent and the level thus attained was termed by Batson the 'Effective Minimum Level' (EML).

The PDL provides a conservative indication of the amount of poverty in a community. It assumes that income is wisely allocated among alternative uses. But 'because the poor do not and cannot budget in the wisest possible way, and because they cannot restrict their expenditure purely to the minimum items, in any community the amount of poverty present will be greater than that suggested by merely taking the proportion of households whose income falls below the Secondary Poverty Datum Line'.[57]

In this study the PDL technique is used to measure the incidence of poverty in the Durban African community. A brief description of the calculation of the PDL is contained in chapter 2 and a comparison with household income and expenditure in 1959 is made, while in chapter 6 the position in 1971 is discussed. However, the shortcomings of the PDL are realized, hence the evaluation, taking into account recent thoughts on concepts of poverty, in chapter 6.

NOTES AND REFERENCES

1 See, for example, Akin L. Mabogunje, *Urbanization in Nigeria*, London: University of London Press, 1968.

2 Cf. the recent articles by J. B. Knight, 'Rural–Urban Income Comparisons and Migration in Ghana', *Bulletin of the Oxford University Institute of Economics and Statistics*, vol. 34 no. 2, 1972, pp. 199–228, and R. T. Bell, 'Migrant Labour: Theory and Policy', *South African Journal of Economics*, vol. 40 no. 4, December 1972, pp. 337–360.

3 Michael P. Todaro, 'Income Expectations, Rural–Urban Migration and Employment in Africa', *International Labour Review*, vol. 104 no. 5, November 1971, p. 391.

4 Marvin P. Miracle & Sara S. Berry, 'Migrant Labour and Economic Development', *Oxford Economic Papers*, vol. 22 no. 1, March 1970, pp. 86–108.

5 Elliot J. Berg, 'The Economics of the Migrant Labour System', in Hilda Kuper (ed.), *Urbanization and Migration in West Africa*, Berkeley and Los Angeles: University of California Press, 1965.

6 Bell, op. cit., pp. 339–41.

7 Knight, op. cit., p. 224.

8 Bell, op. cit., p. 342.

9 Todaro, op. cit.,

10 John C. Caldwell, *African Rural–Urban Migration: The Movement to Ghana's Towns*, Canberra: Australian National University Press, 1969, chapter 4.

11 For a treatment of this subject see, *inter alia*, C. R. Frank, Jr., 'Urban Unemployment and Economic Growth in Africa', *Oxford Economic Papers*, vol. 18 no. 2, July 1968, pp. 250–74, and Michael P. Todaro, 'A Model of Labour Migration and Urban Unemployment in Less Developed Countries', *American Economic Review*, vol. 59 no. 1, March 1969, pp. 138–48.

12 See Knight, op. cit., for an excellent discussion of these problems.

13 John R. Harris & Michael P. Todaro, 'Migration, Unemployment and Development: A Two-Sector Analysis', *American Economic Review*, vol. 60 no. 1, March 1970, pp. 126–42.

14 Todaro, 'Income Expectations . . .', pp. 395–410.

15 Ibid., p. 394.

16 The informal sector is discussed in: International Labour Office, *Employment, Incomes and Equality: A Strategy for Increasing Productive Employment in Kenya*, Geneva 1972, chapters 13 and 22, and Keith Hart, 'Informal Income Opportunities and the Structure of Urban Employment in Ghana', paper presented at the Conference on Urban Unemployment in Africa, Institute of Development Studies, University of Sussex, Brighton, September 1971 (mimeographed).

17 ILO, op. cit., p. 224

18 Ibid., p. 225.

19 Hart, op. cit., p. 1.

20 Ibid., pp. 7–8.

21 Ibid., p. 30.

22 ILO, op. cit., p. 5.

23 For a discussion of these problems, see Caldwell, op. cit.

24 Hart, op. cit., p. 27.

25 Paul Andrew, Malcolm Christie & Richard Martin, 'Squatters and the Evolution of a Lifestyle', *Architectural Design*, vol. 43 no. 1, January 1973, p. 17.

26 ILO, op. cit., pp. 198–9.

27 William A. Hance, *Population, Migration and Urbanization in Africa*, New York: Columbia University Press, 1970, p. 223.

28 All population figures in this section are obtained from the 1965 *Statistical Year Book* and Report 02-05-01 of the 1970 Population Census—*Population of Cities, Towns and Rural Areas* (all published by the Government Printer, Pretoria).

29 J. L. Sadie, 'An Evaluation of Demographic Data Pertaining to the non-White Population of South Africa', *South African Journal of Economics*, vol. 38 no. 2, June 1970, p. 186.

30 G. V. Doxey, *The Industrial Colour Bar in South Africa*, Cape Town: Oxford University Press, 1961, p. 164.

31 Ibid., p. 188.

32 Muriel Horrell, *A Survey of Race Relations in South Africa*, Johannesburg: South African Institute of Race Relations (annual), 1963 p. 124 ff., 1969 pp. 148–50, 1970 pp. 87–8 and 165–6.

33 Subsequently amended by Acts No. 29 of 1956, 49 of 1962 and 56 of 1965, and consolidated by Act No. 36 of 1966 which in turn was amended by Act No. 69 of 1969.

34 For an analysis of the implications of this Act for Durban, see Leo Kuper, Hilstan Watts & Ronald Davies, *Durban: A Study in Racial Ecology*, London: Jonathan Cape, 1958.

35 All population figures in this section are obtained from the City of Durban *Mayor's Minute* (annual) and official census publications.

36 Merle Lipton, 'The South African Census and the Bantustan Policy', *The World Today*, vol. 28 no. 6, June 1972, p. 259.

37 John R. Burrows, The Population and Labour Resources of Natal, Pietermaritzburg: Natal Town and Regional Planning Commission, 1969, p. 171.

38 Ibid., pp. 176–83.

39 For an historical description of early African housing in Durban see: Institute for Social Research, University of Natal, *Baumannville*, Cape Town: Oxford University Press, 1959, pp. 1–3.

40 Hance, op. cit., pp. 270–1.

41 Institute for Social Research, op. cit., p. 2

42 Ibid., p. 1.

43 The colourful rickshas drawn by Africans were at one time a major means of transport in Durban. However, with the advent of the motor vehicle their numbers declined, for example, from 15 209 in 1927 to 8 452 in 1933. Today there are 20 operating on the beachfront where they are purely a tourist attraction, and a further 40 transporting market goods in the city. 'Togt' labourers are casual workers, usually on a daily basis.

44 Unless otherwise indicated all statistics in this section are obtained from the City of Durban *Mayor's Minute* (annual).

45 Much of this discussion is based on: Department of Economics, University of Natal, *The Durban Housing Survey*, Pietermaritzburg: University of Natal Press, 1952, especially chapters 11 and 12.

46 Ibid., pp. 363–4.

47 Through the Prevention of Illegal Squatting Act No. 52 of 1951.

48 See Kuper et al., op. cit., pp. 185–7 and especially footnote 2, p. 186. That this area was to be given over to White occupation was subsequently confirmed by a Group Areas proclamation dated 8 June 1958.

49 Ultimately proposed to cover an area of 2 941 acres and to provide housing for approximately 120 000 persons.

50 Hance, op. cit., p. 288. See also Mabogunje, op. cit., p. 302 for an account of the position in Lagos.

51 Peter Marris, *Family and Social Change in an African City—A Study of Rehousing in Lagos*, Evanston, Ill.: Northwestern University Press, 1962, p. 130.

52 S. J. Prais & H. S. Houthakker, *The Analysis of Family Budgets*, Cambridge: Cambridge University Press, 1955.

53 See: Charles Booth, *Life and Labour of the People in London*, London: Macmillan and Co. Ltd., 17 vol., 1892–7, and B. Seebohm Rowntree, *Poverty: A Study of Town Life*, London: Macmillan & Co. Ltd., 1902.

54 E. Batson, *Social Survey of Cape Town*, Reports Nos. SS 1–30, School of Social Science and Social Administration, University of Cape Town, 1941.

55 A. L. Bowley & A. R. Burnett-Hurst, *Livelihood and Poverty*, London: P. F. King & Son, 1915.

56 E. Batson, *Social Survey of Cape Town*, Report No. SS 212, 'The Poverty Datum Line in March 1952', University of Cape Town, 1952, p. 1.

57 H. L. Watts, *The Poverty Datum Line in Three Cities and Four Towns in South Africa*, Durban: Institute for Social Research, University of Natal, 1967, p. 25.

PART I

CATO MANOR

by

A. S. B. HUMPHREYS, S. S. COOPPAN and ZBIGNIEW A.
KONCZACKI with JOHN R. BURROWS

CHAPTER 2

Poverty in Shantytown

The removal of the shack dwellers from Cato Manor and other areas to KwaMashu commenced in 1958. During that year the Native Administration Department[1] of the Durban Corporation undertook a socio-economic survey of the shack areas in order to establish the amount and type of accommodation required in KwaMashu. The Corporation then requested us to conduct a budget study so as to assess the rent-paying capacity of African families in Durban, and this was completed in the following year. The 1958 study obtained information from 17 900 shack households of which all but 560 were in Cato Manor. In contrast the 1959 survey covered households in the older townships of Lamont and Umlazi Glebe, and the newly established KwaMashu as well as in Cato Manor.

For the purposes of this study we shall, however, confine our attention mainly to the shack dwellers of Cato Manor. The reasons for doing this are several: Cato Manor housed the most recently urbanized community at the time, it had a flourishing informal sector, and its population was in the process of being resettled.

FIELD PROBLEMS

Both surveys encountered severe field problems. Whilst some of these problems were peculiar to the political, social and economic climate prevailing in Cato Manor at the time, others were probably a reflection of more common difficulties in conducting fieldwork on a scientific basis in shack areas.

One of these difficulties relates to statistical sampling methods. In any shack area it is usually impossible to obtain an accurate estimate of the population. However, according to the most reliable estimates Cato Manor contained a population of approximately 120 000 in 1958. In the Corporation survey no attempt at scientific sampling was made; household heads were merely required to assemble at certain fixed points at specified times to provide the relevant information. In the event the households covered contained almost 80 000 persons, or approximately two-thirds of the population.

We attempted to approach the budget study on a more scientific basis but encountered numerous obstacles. The initial lack of relevant data made it impossible to obtain a representative stratified sample of the population by size of household, by household income and by rental categories. A pilot study was therefore conducted at Ntabashishi, an uncontrolled shack area outside the Emergency Camp, to determine the practicability of applying a procedure for stratified sampling utilizing the information available from the larger 1958 survey. The experience gained at Ntabashishi indicated that it would not be possible to follow a prearranged system of stratified sampling in Cato Manor for three reasons, viz. (i) the high mobility of the shack population (especially in the uncontrolled shack areas outside the Emergency Camp); (ii) the demolition of shacks by the local authority which generated suspicion of the purpose of the survey and led to a reluctance to co-operate on the part of many householders; and (iii) the absence from home of many of the adult members of the households during working hours, especially in the smaller households of two or three persons. Moreover, no detailed ground plans showing the distribution of shacks were available, and thus we were unable to select a stratified sample of households.

In consequence, the sample of households obtained was largely determined by householders who were prepared to co-operate and were available for sustained interviews. However, fieldworkers were specifically directed to cover different sizes of households in the course of their inquiries with a view to maintaining relatively the same proportions as those covered in the Durban Corporation survey. This was substantially achieved. An effort was also made to ensure that the sample included, as far as possible, a representative selection from each rental category. Preliminary inquiries established that the overwhelming majority of rentals in Cato Manor ranged between R2 and R3,50 per month, and consequently over 80 per cent of the households interviewed fell into this range.

Because it was not feasible to carry out any statistical sampling procedure in the budget study, no standard error could be calculated; however, the sample ultimately contained 20 per cent of the estimated population. Other studies of urban communities in Africa have also encountered sampling problems. In a study in Lagos, for example, scientific sampling was hindered by inaccurate lists, inexperienced interviewers and changes or delays in government plans.[2] But the view has been expressed that 'pragmatically, if we are willing to go beyond the strict logic of our method, a combination of sampling techniques and descriptive analysis will reinforce each other'.[3]

Cato Manor consisted of a number of 'localities' of uneven population density within each of the two broad divisions, viz. the Emergency Camp and the uncontrolled shack areas outside it. Sampling was therefore designed so as to provide a fair geographical stratification, and the households were drawn from six localities, viz. Cabazini, Ezimbuzini, Newclare and Nsimbini in the Emergency Camp, and Banki and Tintown in the adjoining uncontrolled areas[4] (Map 3). Approximately 60 per cent of the Cato Manor population resided in the Emergency Camp in 1958.

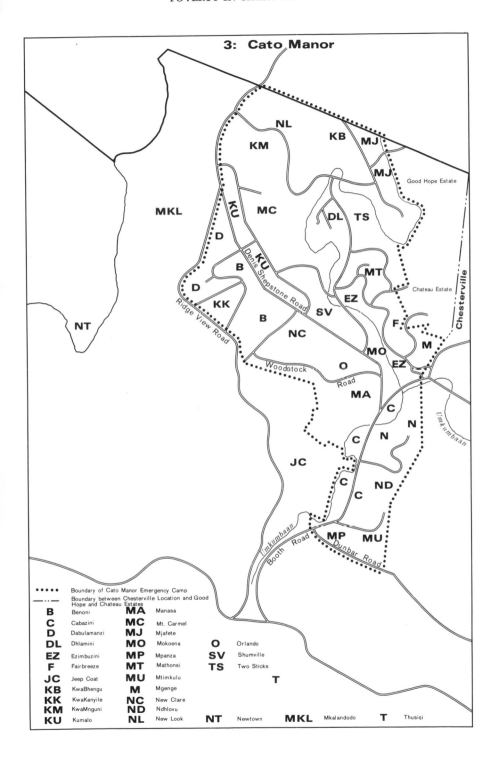

3: Cato Manor

Boundary of Cato Manor Emergency Camp
Boundary between Chesterville Location and Good Hope and Chateau Estates

B	Benoni	**MA**	Manasa			
C	Cabazini	**MC**	Mt. Carmel			
D	Dabulamanzi	**MJ**	Mjafete			
DL	Dhlamini	**MO**	Mokoena	**O**	Orlando	
EZ	Ezimbuzini	**MP**	Mpanza	**SV**	Shumville	
F	Fairbreeze	**MT**	Mathonsi	**TS**	Two Sticks	
JC	Jeep Coat	**MU**	Mtimkulu			
KB	KwaBhengu	**M**	Mgenge	**T**		
KK	KwaKanyile	**NC**	New Clare			
KM	KwaMnguni	**ND**	Ndhlovu			
KU	Kumalo	**NL**	New Look	**NT** Newtown	**MKL** Mkalandodo	**T** Thusini

The political and social climate prevailing in Cato Manor also affected the fieldwork, which was undertaken in the most difficult circumstances at a time of great tension. The Durban Corporation was in the process of demolishing shacks and either transferring families to new accommodation at KwaMashu or repatriating those not legally entitled to reside within the municipal area to the Reserves. The accompanying resentment and uncertainty among Cato Manor residents resulted in a considerable amount of resistance being encountered, particularly as the unavoidable employment of Durban Corporation personnel as fieldworkers led to the association of the University investigation in the minds of the local residents with the Corporation's rehousing programme. These tensions culminated in serious disturbances in June 1959 which led to the suspension, and shortly thereafter the complete abandonment, of all fieldwork in Cato Manor.

A further source of resistance arose from the fact that a considerable amount of unlicensed private trading was being conducted in the African residential areas. In Cato Manor, in particular, illicit liquor sales were prevalent over the week-ends. Consequently there was a reluctance to disclose information to fieldworkers which it was feared might find its way to the law-enforcement authorities. At times, conscious efforts were made to suppress information on expenditure which might have caused liquor brewing to be suspected as an illegal source of supplementary income. Even if fieldworkers observed such activities, their attempts to establish the amounts of supplementary income generated from these sources proved of no avail. In fact, their probings into details of such income and expenditure heightened suspicion and even provoked hostility on the part of some residents.

Trading activities during week-ends at Cato Manor[5] increased the difficulties of interviewing and on occasions even made it dangerous for the field teams. Of necessity, a great deal of work had to be concentrated into the week-ends. Aside from interviewing housewives to obtain details of the previous day's (Saturday's) expenditure, which would normally occupy a full day, advantage also had to be taken of the presence at home of heads of households in order to obtain details of their own personal expenditure and to confirm from them, as far as possible, the accuracy of the information supplied by housewives during the week. On Sundays, interviewing was restricted to the morning, and even then many respondents were not readily available because of church attendance and other activities. Sunday afternoons were normally given over to recreation and relaxation, and the intrusion of fieldworkers was unwelcome. Moreover, the reluctance of male heads of households to discuss their incomes and personal expenditure in the presence of their wives also necessitated their being interviewed separately at week-ends.

DEMOGRAPHIC ANALYSIS

The core of the African housing problem in South African cities comprises families which are, notwithstanding official policy, a permanent and integral part of the urban population. Any poverty and housing study must, therefore, be concerned primarily with this section of the population rather than with the more 'floating' population of single persons.

The test therefore applied in the selection of households was a practical residential one, viz. those families in which all members were, at the time of the survey, living in Durban under the same roof and sharing a common table.[6] Married migratory labourers, i.e. single-person households which comprised men or women living in the urban area but having spouses and/or other dependants in the Reserves, were excluded. (A separate analysis of one-person households is, however, presented later in this chapter.) Also excluded were those families which might be regarded as 'transitional urban families', some of whose members lived in Durban and others in the Reserves.

HOUSEHOLD DATA

The arithmetic mean (or 'average') size of household in the 1959 budget study was 4,3 persons. This is only fractionally lower than the 4,4 persons which was later established by the Durban Corporation as the average size of families moved from the shack areas during the period 1958–65. In contrast the older settlements of Lamont and Umlazi Glebe were characterized by larger average-sized households of 5,8 and 6,1 persons respectively.

Despite the unsettled conditions in which most of them lived, household heads were mainly Durban residents of long standing. Only one-tenth had resided in Durban for less than five years, while almost three-quarters had lived in the city for ten years or more, the median length of residence of all household heads being fourteen years.

THE ECONOMICALLY ACTIVE POPULATION

The work potential and ability of a community to support itself is largely determined, in the first instance, by its age and sex structure. In this respect the Corporation survey faced snags in that the ages of two-fifths of the females (mainly housewives in the 15–60 years age group) were not recorded in the original data. Moreover, there were a large number of male heads of households whose ages were unspecified, with the result that the ages of almost 25 per cent of the sample were unspecified.

Age recording was, however, more accurate in the case of younger persons, and 42 per cent were under 15 years of age. In the budget study, no difficulties regarding age reporting were encountered, and 44 per cent were under 15 years. Thus, in both surveys, more than two out of five persons were below what is normally accepted as working age.[7] This situation corresponded closely to the overall position in Natal where, in 1960, 43 per cent of the African population were under 15 years of age.

An important feature which has an obvious bearing on later sections of this study is the large number of potential dependants who had to be supported by income producers; only 53 per cent of the population in the budget study were aged 15–64 years or, in other words, were in the age groups normally regarded as 'economically active'.

A further factor limiting the earning capacity of the population was the relatively large proportion of women. The ratio between the sexes is normally measured by the masculinity rate, which is the number of males in the population per 100 females. The masculinity rate in the Corporation survey was only 88,6 and in the budget study 90, compared with 94 for Whites in the Durban metropolitan area in 1960.[8] The economic significance of a low masculinity rate is that it increases the proportion of dependants to income producers and lowers both the average wage earnings per head of population and average earnings of workers. In the African community the position was further exacerbated by the fact that most women either did not work at all or earned only small amounts.

In Cato Manor the work participation rate (WPR)[9] was 93,7 for men and 16,3 for women. The overall WPR was 50,8, and this resulted in a dependency ratio of 1:2,3. Thus the male WPR revealed a fairly full utilization of potential labour, but only a small proportion of the female work potential was being utilized. Almost all the wage-earners were in regular employment, only a small minority being engaged in casual or temporary jobs.

The occupational distribution in the budget study showed that 74 per cent of the male workers in Cato Manor were engaged in manual work, mainly as 'labourers'—a term which is widely used in studies of employment and earnings but which tends to be an omnibus category which obscures real differences in occupations. In the other areas the comparable figure ranged from 48–68 per cent, the difference probably being explained by the higher rentals in municipal housing schemes which attracted the better-paid workers from more skilled occupations. So far as female employment was concerned, almost four-fifths were in domestic service.

HOUSEHOLD INCOME

Three main sources of income were disclosed by the shack households, viz. (i) wages and salaries; (ii) rentals from tenants; and (iii) pensions, welfare grants and allowances.

Wage income constituted by far the most important source of household income. The 1959 budget study showed that the median male wage in Cato Manor was R5,20 per week, which was approximately one-third lower than that in the municipal townships. The median wage for female workers was only R1,60 per week, and this reflected the low wages earned in domestic service.

Because of the importance of wage income the number of wage-earners per household was the major factor in determining the level of household income. Over three-quarters of all households had only one worker, and an analysis of the incomes of secondary earners showed that they averaged only one-third that of the primary earner. This is largely because most of the secondary earners were women, who received much lower wages than men. Thus the importance of the primary earner was clearly illustrated.

The median weekly household wage income in Cato Manor was R5,60, and again this was approximately one-third below the level in the other areas. This difference can be attributed to two main factors. First, the average number of wage-earners per household was lower in the shack areas than elsewhere, and second, the greater proportion of male workers in Cato Manor were in lower-paid occupations.

The fundamental importance of wage income to the community is shown by the fact that whereas median household wage income in Cato Manor was R5,60 per week median total household income was only slightly higher at R6,10.

Non-wage income accrued to only a comparatively small proportion of households; it was relatively most important in Cato Manor where it contributed to the incomes of approximately 27 per cent of all households, or more than double the proportion found in the townships.

By far the most important source of non-wage income was rent received from letting rooms to tenants or subtenants. However, the practice of room-letting was not as widespread as might have been expected. The reason for this was that over three-quarters of the household heads were themselves 'tenants' in the sense that they rented rooms from the Indian landowner or the African 'owner–occupier'. They thus occupied only a portion of the shack and had no additional accommodation available for subletting. Only 2 per cent of this group sublet rooms. Of the 'owner–occupiers' it was only those from the African-owned areas of Chateau and Good Hope Estates (which had been purchased by Africans in 1930–1) who were landowners. The majority were only 'owners' in the sense that they were the original builders or occupants of their dwellings. Among this group the incidence of room-letting was very large, more than 94 per cent receiving income from this source. Overall, however, only 21 per cent of households in Cato Manor let rooms. In contrast, while most of the households in Lamont, Umlazi Glebe and KwaMashu owned the dwellings they were occupying, less than 10 per cent took in tenants.

This source was almost always a supplement to wage income and seldom provided the sole means of support. The most common rent paid by tenants for a room in Cato Mano was about R3 per month (or just under 70 cents per week) and, since most landlords took in two or three tenants rather than only one—on average there were 2,8 subtenants per household—the average rent received by landlords was approximately R1,70 per week.

No information was recorded concerning the standard of housing and the only data available related to whether the shack dwelling was exclusively occupied by a given household or whether it was shared by two or more households. It was found that about 90 per cent of the households were occupying only a portion of the shack in which they were living. Unfortunately, however, this type of information is of limited value in the absence of precise details regarding the size of dwellings.

The marked discrepancy between the median wage incomes of Cato Manor, on the one hand, and the three established municipal townships, on the other hand, has already been noted. The Cato Manor households were, however, able to make up some of the gap by means of non-wage income, although their median total income from all sources still remained considerably less than that of the other three areas.

Apart from wage income and rent from room-letting, there were few other disclosed sources of income. Few households received supplementary income in the form of pensions, welfare grants or other allowances, and for the community as a whole these additional sources of revenue were of negligible importance.

THE EXTENT OF POVERTY

The concept and components of the PDL have already been mentioned in chapter 1. The PDL is calculated separately for each household and is determined by the size of the household and the age, sex and activity of its members. Because of the variations in these factors there is a range of PDL costs for each size of household in a community; for example, it was found that PDL costs for four-person households in the sample ranged from R17 to R44 per month.

The costing of the PDL is a time-consuming task, involving lengthy observation of the buying habits of the particular community. In 1958 a detailed PDL investigation in Durban was undertaken and the minimum required quantities in respect of each of the primary components were estimated.[10] Food is the major component of the PDL in terms of costs; the diet adopted in this study was based on that compiled for White and Coloured families by the South African National Nutrition Council.[11] This body also provided the scale for assessing the cost of food for adults, adolescents and children, taking into account not only the age and sex of the individual but also, in the case of adults, their degree of activity as determined by their occupations.

While the constituents which comprise the food component of the PDL can be estimated on a physiological basis, and have consequently been fairly precisely determined by scientific research into nutrition, the constituents of the clothing component are largely determined by social considerations and personal preferences and must necessarily be of an arbitrary nature. Cleansing materials for personal and household use were costed on the basis of estimated minimum requirements. With the growth of the city, opportunities for collecting fuel from the neighbouring bush had receded, and as a result the majority of families purchased firewood in small bundles which were consumed in a few days. Coal was usually bought in small quantities and lighting was by small oil-lamps or candles.

To the total cost of these basic components must be added transport costs, rent charges and tax payments (all obligatory payments) in order to compute the Secondary PDL. The topography of Durban and the location of Cato Manor vis-à-vis the main industrial areas of the city are such that the majority of shack dwellers were compelled to make use of motor transport to reach their places of work. Absence of information on the distribution of workers according to their areas of employment and by the length of their working week precluded the calculation of a weighted average cost. It was, therefore, necessary to compute an average cost of transport on the assumption that the work places were more or less evenly distributed over the city. Average transport costs per worker (both full-time and part-time) were, therefore, assessed according to the prevailing fares charged from Cato Manor to four major areas of African employment in Durban— Durban Central, Point, Maydon Wharf and Jacobs—by the cheapest form of transport, which was by municipal or private bus service. The small minority which walked to work was unlikely to affect this average figure to any appreciable extent.

The average rent paid by a household for a shack at Cato Manor was 65 cents per week. We have seen that rooms were let at an average rental of 70 cents per week; a household which was able to take in a tenant was therefore able to more than recoup the rental it was paying for its shack.

The rate of taxation used was that prevailing for Africans in 1958, i.e. a poll-tax at R2 per annum for all males aged 18 years and over. Exemptions were found to be rare and therefore this possibility was disregarded. Since this survey excluded men with wives in the Reserves, the hut-tax of R1 per annum per wife payable in those areas was not applicable.

The primary purpose of a PDL study is to ascertain the extent of poverty in a community, and this is done by comparing the income and PDL for each household. Rather than comparing total household income with the PDL, however, we used wage income only. This was done for two main reasons. First, the information on non-wage income was not as reliable as that on wages, and it was suspected that non-wage income was, for various reasons, often withheld or not fully disclosed. Second, from the viewpoint of the individual household non-wage income tended to be less dependable as a source of income than wages, particularly in view of the impending clearance of all shack areas. For example, the most important disclosed source of non-wage income was rent received from tenants, but with their removal to new townships the Cato Manor households would no longer be able to rely upon this source to supplement their incomes. It so happened, however, that the median value of total disclosed household income was only 60 cents per week higher than median household wage income and was therefore of minor significance.

The median PDL cost for Cato Manor households amounted to R7,35 per week compared with median household wage income of R5,60 per week, thus leaving a shortfall of R1,75 per week. However, it was also necessary to examine the effects of the impending resettlement upon the rent-paying capacity of the Cato Manor residents. This, in effect, entailed assessing the adequacy of their available residual income to meet the current rental charges at KwaMashu, as well as the additional transport costs involved. The average weighted rental payable at KwaMashu was R6,50 per month (inclusive of water charges and school levy), or R1,50 per week. But only 24 per cent of Cato Manor households had an excess of income over PDL costs adequate to meet this rental together with the additional transport cost of 45 cents[12] per week which was incurred by residents of Kwa-Mashu because of the greater distances from places of employment in the city.

THE POSITION OF ONE-PERSON HOUSEHOLDS

Households consisting of only one person have so far been excluded from this discussion. However, the survey included a sample of single people of whom three-quarters were men. Almost nine-tenths of the men were unmarried, while only 50 per cent of the women had never married, one-third were widowed and the rest had been married, divorced or deserted.

These single persons were mostly tenants, occupying a part of someone else's shack. Many of them had resided in Durban for a considerable time; 36 per cent had resided there for periods varying between 10 and 20 years, and 16 per cent for 20 years or more. The distribution of single persons according to district of origin showed that almost 90 per cent came from districts within Natal, the largest proportion (43 per cent) coming from the coastal region. These figures accord very closely with those relating to African males registered in Durban in 1957–8, the corresponding proportions being 81 per cent and 48 per cent.[13] Over nine-tenths of the men and two-thirds of the women were employed, mainly in manual occupations.

Wages were by far the most important source of income. The median monthly income of all single men (including those receiving no wages) amounted to R20,68, of which only 10 cents was derived from other sources. In the case of women only 80 cents of the total median income of R7,44 emanated from other sources. The principal source of income apart from wages consisted of rentals received from tenants. This was an insignificant source of income among men but was somewhat more important in the case of women, 10 per cent of whom took in tenants.

Most of the males (88 per cent) had incomes exceeding their PDL, whereas 70 per cent of the females, due to their smaller recorded incomes and greater unemployment rate, had a shortfall. It should be pointed out, however, that the money wage of those in domestic service excludes other benefits such as food rations.

Thus, according to the criteria adopted in this survey single men were the only group having a median income exceeding PDL costs. As a corollary, only single men as a group had the ability to pay the higher rentals at KwaMashu.

EXPENDITURE PATTERNS

The budget survey naturally involved the collection of household expenditure data. This information was obtained on an annual, monthly, weekly or daily basis, depending upon the nature of the items and upon the ability of the householder to provide the required information over a longer or shorter time period.

Thus, for example, it was found that more reliable information regarding expenditure on durable goods such as furniture, hardware and transport equipment, as well as on clothing, medical care, fines, tax payments, etc., could be obtained on an annual basis. Not only were payments on certain of these items made annually, but respondents more readily recalled sums disbursed on such items in terms of annual expenditure. Moreover, since the acquisition of items such as furniture, hardware, transport equipment and clothing usually involved the expenditure of relatively large sums if paid for in cash, their incidence could be spread over the annual period without distorting the general pattern of expenditure in any one week or month.

A monthly or weekly basis was adopted in respect of rentals, expenditure on education, remittances, church contributions, insurance, savings and borrowings. Payments on these items were customarily made on a quarterly, monthly or weekly basis and could thus be more easily recalled by respondents. In respect of certain other items, however, expenditure was recorded on a daily basis, making allowances for cash as well as credit purchases. These items included food, cigarettes and tobacco, fuel and light, laundry and cleansing materials, transport, amusement, recreation, sport and reading matter.

Expenditure figures obtained on an annual and monthly basis were then reduced to a weekly basis to facilitate comparison with incomes since the majority of wage-earners were paid on a weekly basis.

Median expenditure on food in Cato Manor was R7,00 per week

and on all PDL components R10,15 per week. These figures substantiate the generally observed consumption pattern of low-income groups where the bulk of income is spent on food. Households generally spent far more on PDL components than the amount which it was estimated would be sufficient to purchase their minimum requirements.

Food was a slightly more important element of expenditure than it was of estimated PDL costs in Cato Manor. Thus, whereas food was allowed 68 per cent of the total estimated cost of all PDL components, it accounted for over 69 per cent of actual expenditure on these components. Moreover, while households spent on all PDL components 38 per cent more than the cost of their estimated requirements, their expenditure on food was 40 per cent higher than the estimated cost of their food requirements.

In Cato Manor median expenditure on PDL items amounted to R10,15 compared with the median PDL of R7,35. In KwaMashu the respective figures were R12,30 and R9,80, in Lamont R10,70 and R10,50 and in Umlazi Glebe R12,10 and R10,80.

Despite the fact that the majority of households surveyed were not in receipt of a wage income sufficient to cover the estimated cost of PDL components, they were able to live above the PDL in respect of these six components and, moreover, were able to purchase these components from day to day on a cash basis. In Cato Manor 86 per cent of the households incurred weekly expenditure which exceeded their weekly wage incomes, compared with 68–80 per cent for the other three areas. We have noted that, for the vast majority of households, wages constituted the sole source of income and, for the rest, declared non-wage income formed only a small fraction of total household income. It appears, therefore, that the actual or apparent income of most households was higher than their declared wage income, implying access to undisclosed sources of supplementary income.

The Cato Manor community had the highest apparent income from non-wage or undisclosed sources; this permitted it to attain a moderate level of expenditure despite its low wage income. Lamont, on the other hand, while having a much higher level of wage income than Cato Manor, spent approximately the same amount on PDL components and thus showed the lowest apparent non-wage or undisclosed income. KwaMashu and Umlazi Glebe, although having relatively high median wage incomes, showed an expenditure which was considerably higher than wage income.

The principal finding of this comparison between wage income and expenditure on PDL items has been the apparent existence of relatively substantial quantities of undisclosed income which made expenditure of this magnitude possible. Thus far, the only measure of the relative sufficiency of the shack dwellers' income has been the comparison between wage income and the estimated and actual expenditure on PDL components. The PDL concept, however, represents a most severe standard by which to assess a household's requirements and omits many items which are necessary to maintain modern urban standards. When actual expenditure incurred on additional items such as beverages, furniture and household equipment, medical and educational expenses, tobacco and liquor, remittances to families in the Reserves, insurance, house repairs, etc., is added to expenditure on the PDL components, the extent of undisclosed supplementary income is found to be of even greater magnitude. The distribution of household expenditure in Cato Manor among various items is shown in Table 2:1.

Table 2.1

PERCENTAGE MEAN ANNUAL HOUSEHOLD EXPENDITURE BY ITEM AND AREA

Item	All areas	Cato Manor	Kwa-Mashu	Lamont	Umlazi Glebe
Food and beverages	50,3	55,3	45,3	54,7	51,1
Cigarettes and tobacco	3,5	3,7	3,2	3,5	3,5
Fuel and light	4,9	3,6	5,0	6,7	6,0
Laundry and cleansing	2,0	2,0	1,7	2,1	2,0
Personal care	0,7	0,6	0,6	0,4	0,9
Transport	7,4	6,9	8,1	6,5	6,6
Recreation and sport	1,5	1,7	1,6	1,0	0,9
Tax	0,3	0,3	0,3	0,3	0,3
Rent	7,0	5,0	8,9	6,5	7,3
Householders' purchases	3,3	2,5	3,9	3.1	3,4
Clothing and footwear	8,0	8,9	7,4	7,2	7,9
Furniture and household equipment	6,5	3,9	9,6	3,6	5,8
Musical instruments and records	0,5	0,4	0,6	0,4	0,5
Transport equipment	0,5	0,9	0,4	0,2	0,1
Education	1,0	1,0	0,7	1,3	1,2
Medical care	1,2	1,9	0,9	0,8	0,7
Fines	0,2	0,3	0,2	0,1	0,1
Church and clubs	0,4	0,3	0,4	0,6	0,5
Insurance	0,7	0,4	0,6	1,0	0,8
Other	0,2	0,1	0,4	0,1	0,3
Total	100,0	100,0	100,0	100,0	100,0
Mean Annual Expenditure (R)	736,2	682,8	826,0	659,6	745,4
Mean Annual Income (R)	410,4	332,4	448,6	465,8	474,6
Mean Household Size (persons)	4,9	4,3	4,9	5,9	6,1

EFFECTS OF RESETTLEMENT

The expenditure patterns in the three municipal townships are also included in Table 2:1 since they point to some interesting differences between these areas and the shack settlements and enable us to ascertain the effects of resettlement on budgetary allocations.

As will be apparent from the table, the group *food and beverages* claimed by far the largest proportion of total expenditure, comprising over 50 per cent in three of the four areas. The overall proportion of expenditure devoted to food was higher than among urban Africans in Southern Rhodesia in 1958–9, where budget studies disclosed that food purchases accounted for 46 per cent of cash outlays.[14] The lower proportion in KwaMashu is explained mainly by the fact that expenditure on transport, rent and furniture was higher in this township than in the others, both in terms of value and as a proportion of total expenditure. Thus, although the absolute value of expenditure on food did not differ significantly in KwaMashu compared with other townships, it was proportionately less.

The differences in *transport* costs between the different areas were found to be fairly substantial. Expenditure in KwaMashu (the highest) was in fact 57 per cent higher than expenditure in Lamont (the lowest).[15] KwaMashu residents paid more in *rent* than residents in the other areas, Cato Manor being the lowest in this case. It is obvious from this why there was so much objection on the part of Cato Manor residents to being moved to KwaMashu. Both their rents and transport costs would be increased substantially as a result of the move. Average rents in KwaMashu were 116 per cent higher, while average bus fares were 70 per cent higher, than in Cato Manor.

Expenditure on *furniture and household equipment* was not an important item in Cato Manor. However, a comparison with the position obtaining in KwaMashu at the time is interesting. KwaMashu households were spending almost 10 per cent of their expenditure on furniture compared with only 4 per cent in Cato Manor. This was a direct effect of resettlement. On moving to new accommodation, many households had acquired considerable quantities of furniture, some spending as much as R480 during the previous year. This reported expenditure may, however, be questioned on two grounds. First, a large proportion of furniture was acquired through hire-purchase agreements. It was not always clear whether the reported annual expenditure on furniture and household equipment was, in fact, the original full price of the articles, which may have been paid for in instalments over a period of up to two years. Second, it was reported that many households at KwaMashu purchased excessive quantities of new furniture for prestige purposes and were subsequently unable to meet their monthly instalments. In such cases, the furniture was recovered by the seller and the recorded expenditure of the household might not have reflected this suspension of payment. For these reasons the average figures of expenditure on furniture were not considered to be wholly reliable.

About 80 per cent of the households incurred expenditure on *medical care*. The average expenditure on medical care in Cato Manor was twice as high as that in the three municipal townships. This might perhaps be attributed to the unhygienic conditions caused by poor sanitation and overcrowding at Cato Manor, and also to its closer proximity to the King Edward VIII Hospital, resulting in greater use being made of hospital facilities by the shack community.

More than one-half of the households contributed to their *church* and similarly over one-half reported expenditure on *education*. The average weekly expenditure of 14 cents recorded at Cato Manor was slightly lower than in the municipal townships because of the lower average number of schoolchildren per shack household.

Some 45 per cent of the households stated that they sent regular or occasional *remittances* to the Reserves. The highest average weekly expenditure on remittances was recorded at Cato Manor (57 cents); this was less than 10 per cent of median income and was much lower than the 20–25 per cent of earnings remitted to the Reserves in other studies. This might be regarded as evidence of a lower degree of urbanization as it appeared that the Cato Manor community had a larger proportion of dependants still living in the Reserves than any of the other areas.

Comparatively few households reported any expenditure on *insurance*. About one-third of the households in the older townships— Lamont and Umlazi Glebe —were paying insurance premiums, the figure falling to 25 per cent at KwaMashu and 14 per cent at Cato Manor. Households in the three established townships paid an average of 11 cents per week in premiums as against 7 cents at Cato Manor, and since the dwellings rented in the townships were already insured by the Durban Corporation, the expenditure must have consisted mainly of premiums on personal insurances of various kinds.

Only one-tenth of the households reported any expenditure on the *repairs* or improvement of their dwellings, and of these the great majority were resident at KwaMashu. Many of the householders at KwaMashu carried out various improvements to their homes after moving in, such as plastering and painting walls and adding doors. As we shall see in chapter 4, various studies have shown that occupants of informal sector housing make gradual improvements to their dwellings. However, this was apparently not the case in Cato Manor, the resettlement policy not making it worth the occupants' while to effect improvements.

The balance of the more significant items shown in Table 2:1 did not vary substantially from one area to another, with the exception of *fuel and light*. In Cato Manor expenditure on this item was lower, both absolutely and relatively, than in the municipal townships. This was a direct result of the nature of shack dwellings. Comparatively few households had a separate kitchen or a stove; cooking was essentially informal, usually over an open fire, and was often conducted on a communal basis with households from neighbouring shacks sharing a fire in order to economize on fuel.

What stands out clearly from this analysis is that the policy of

rehousing Africans in townships on the urban periphery involved them
in a significant increase in living-costs. The question that arises here is:
if official mass-housing schemes are introduced ahead of a community's
capacity to pay, who should meet the increased costs in the interim
period? Should society as a whole bear the costs or can the residents
be fairly charged the higher costs before their wages have increased?
The answer surely is that if a section of society deems it necessary to
enforce resettlement it appears only reasonable to expect that section
to bear directly the burden of the increased costs involved. However,
what had in fact happened was that those who were forced to move
were obliged, in the first instance, to carry the greater proportion of
the increased costs. Some employers did, it is true, increase the wage
rates of employees who were affected by the higher living costs in
the new townships, but this too was unsatisfactory since those industries which employed a substantial number of such workers tended to
be affected more than those which employed only a few such workers.
Thus there resulted an uneven distribution of the burden.

THE NEED FOR HIGHER WAGES

Rent-paying capacity, as such, is ultimately dependent upon the
adequacy of wage incomes since, even if illegal income existed, it
could not be an acceptable means of livelihood on either moral or
legal grounds. To take illegal income into consideration (even if it
could be accurately determined) as a factor which raised rent-paying
capacity would be indefensible on any but the most cynical grounds.

The Durban Corporation survey demonstrated that the 1958 wage
levels were adequate to provide only the single male worker with the
essentials of living, i.e. with the basic PDL components. In order to
enable the average African family unit to maintain itself at a PDL
level without having recourse to illegal sources of supplementary
income, to enable it to meet the rentals then being charged in the
townships, and to permit of minimum expenditure on a restricted range
of additional items (such as medical care, education, furniture and
household items, tobacco and liquor) which were judged to be necessary for urban living it was considered that the figure of R12 per week
(or R52 per month) was the minimum wage income which the average
African family should have been receiving in 1959.

This was much lower than the Effective Minimum Level of R16,12
for such a household, but nevertheless appeared as a considerable
increase over the wage levels obtaining at the time. In South Africa
low wages for African labour relative to Whites have tended to become
accepted as the norm. Africans have traditionally occupied the low-
paid unskilled labour categories, have lacked opportunities to progress
to more highly skilled occupations (and therefore to higher levels of
remuneration), and are statutorily prevented from achieving wage
increases through normal trade union channels and collective bargain-

ing procedures. Nor had compulsory cost-of-living allowances or government intervention in the determination of minimum wages enabled African wage incomes to keep abreast of the rise in the cost of living during the 1950s, particularly in the urban areas.[16] Consequently, the great majority of families had a wage income below the 'bread line'.

Thus the survey clearly indicated that the gap between wage income received and the expenditure necessary to maintain an average urban African family on a minimum standard of living had to be bridged by raising wages. Subsequent changes in wages and costs of living during the period 1959–71 are analysed in chapter 6.

The above argument for higher wages is, however, applicable only to those engaged in wage employment, i.e. in the formal sector. But when the existence of the informal (non-wage) sector is recognized two further questions are raised:

1. For families with members engaged in both sectors, is not the promotion of the informal sector a legitimate alternative to raising wages?
2. What policy should be adopted towards those wholly engaged in non-criminal informal sector activities?

In attempting to answer the first point we should distinguish between those cases where the household head is in wage employment but also engaged in informal activities to supplement his income, and those cases where the household head is in wage employment but his wife or some other member of his family is active in the informal sector. If public mass housing for the poor involves them in higher rental payments, it is surely not socially optimal for a household head to be obliged to seek additional employment ('moonlighting') or supplementary sources of income in order to meet the higher rentals. And since much of informal sector activity is irregular and hence does not provide a stable income, we cannot regard the promotion of informal activities as a desirable alternative to raising the wages of the household head in the formal sector.

With regard to the second point, it is clear that incomes could be increased by the encouragement rather than the harassment of certain informal activities. This could be done, for example, by easing some of the licensing restrictions on the activities of petty traders, hawkers and taxi operators, and encouraging the informal construction industry. The promotion of the informal sector would in this sense be complementary to raising wages in the formal sector.

NOTES AND REFERENCES

1 Known as the Bantu Administration Department from 1 February 1959.

2 Peter Marris, 'Motives and Methods: Reflections on a Study in Lagos', in Horace Miner (ed.), *The City in Modern Africa*, London: Pall Mall Press, 1967, pp. 42–3.

3 Ibid., p. 43.

4 Cato Manor consisted of over 50 clearly defined 'localities'. In the Emergency Camp these localities were bounded by roads while in the uncontrolled areas specific clusters of shacks could be defined by a landowners' boundary, a road, a row of trees or a valley. Names often reflected the date of establishment (New Look after the women's fashion of the late 1940s), ethnic groupings (Matatiele, inhabited by Xhosa, after a town in the Transkei), topography (Cabazini—a 'flat place'), an incident (Two Sticks after a stick fight) or some local idiosyncrasy (Raincoat after a rent-collector who wore a brown raincoat, or Ezimbuzini, 'place of the goats').

5 It was authoritatively estimated that the population of Cato Manor was approximately doubled each week-end by an influx of visitors, mainly males, from the single residential quarters provided by the Durban Corporation, from compounds and from licensed residential premises in the city. (See Records of Defence Evidence: Cato Manor Murder Trial: Durban Supreme Court, August 1960.)

6 On the other hand a number of plural households where the marital relationship of the household head was one of cohabitation, were treated as urban families if they complied with the above criterion, i.e. lived in Durban under the same roof and shared a common table.

7 It should be remembered, however, that the sample was partly selected on the basis of qualification for municipal housing, and that for this purpose the migrant and transitional family units, as well as all the single-person households, were removed. The age and sex structure of this population, therefore, would be expected to differ considerably from that of the total African population of Durban (which was greatly distorted by the large number of single male migrant workers temporarily residing in the city) and could be taken as more typical of the population requiring housing in new townships. Of the total African population in the Durban metropolitan area, for example, only 25 per cent was under 15 years of age at the time of the 1960 population census, while the corresponding figure for the White population was 27 per cent.

8 The figure for Africans in the DMA was 152, the difference being due to the presence of single male migrants.

9 The work participation rate used here comprises the number of men (or women) who were reported to be gainfully employed, divided by the total number of men (or women) aged 15 years and over. Work-participation rates are frequently defined in terms of the population aged between 15 and 59 or between 15 and 64, but the open-ended group was preferred here because there were very few persons aged 60 or over in the survey population.

10 Ruth Webb, 'Durban's Poverty Line for 1958', unpublished report of the Department of Economics, University of Natal. A detailed account of the calculation of the PDL may be found in P. N. Pillay, *A Poverty Datum Line Study Among Africans in Durban*, Occasional Paper No. 3, Durban: Department of Economics, University of Natal, 1973.

11 'Adequate Family Diets at Low Cost', Technical Bulletin, Publicity Series No. 8, National Nutrition Council, Department of Public Health of the Union of South Africa, 1947, p. 11.

12 The average transport cost per worker by bus (which was at the time the form of transport used by the great majority of the residents of KwaMashu because of the absence of an adequate commuter rail service) was R4,19 per month. Since there was an average of 1,2 workers per household at Cato Manor and KwaMashu the transport

cost per household amounted to R5,03 per month at KwaMashu as against R3,11 per month at Cato Manor, leaving a difference of R1,92 per month or 45 cents per week, which constituted the additional costs resulting from resettlement.

13 Burrows, op. cit., p. 168.

14 William J. Barber, 'Urbanisation and Economic Growth: The Case of Two White Settler Territories', in Horace Miner (ed.), op. cit., p. 109.

15 The difference is no longer as great because of the subsequent installation of a fast rail service which has lowered the cost of travelling between KwaMashu and places of work.

16 For example, more than 14 years separated successive wage determinations for unskilled labour in Durban.

CHAPTER 3

The Informal Sector

In chapter 1 we noted the existence of a flourishing informal sector in the African shack settlements, while the analysis in chapter 2 revealed the apparent importance of undisclosed sources of income in the budgets of shack households. We now proceed to discuss the discrepancy between disclosed income and expenditure and the role of informal sector activities in bridging this gap.

THE 'DISCLOSED INCOME' DEFICIT

Family budget studies usually reveal an excess of expenditure over income, one of the few exceptions being a study in the then Northern and Southern Rhodesia between 1958 and 1960 which found that the recorded money income of urban African households exceeded recorded expenditure by about 6 per cent.[1]

In Cato Manor almost nine-tenths of the households showed a budgetary deficit, while a comparison of household wage incomes and expenditure showed that only 5 per cent enjoyed an income surplus. Households in Lamont appeared to be relatively better off than those in the remaining areas, 10,1 per cent showing an excess of income over expenditure compared with 4 per cent in Umlazi Glebe and 3,7 per cent in KwaMashu. For most shack households, in fact, the discrepancy between wage income and expenditure was almost as large as the wage income itself.

As has already been indicated, only a small fraction of the discrepancy between expenditure and wage income can be explained by disclosed income from rents, pensions, family allowances, etc. The great bulk of this discrepancy must thus be attributed either to the serious exaggeration of expenditure by informants or to the existence of considerable amounts of undisclosed income, or to a combination of both these factors.

A general tendency for households to exaggerate the amount spent on the various items covered by the survey might be suspected for a number of reasons. First, some households might have wished to exaggerate their expenditure for prestige reasons, especially on certain items of conspicuous consumption such as clothing and furniture. A converse influence which might, to some extent, offset the effects of exaggeration would be the imperfect recollection of past expenditure.

A second factor which might have tended to inflate the expenditure figures was the relative frequency of credit buying, particularly in the case of clothing and consumer durables. This has already been discussed in chapter 2. It should be added, however, that where there is a failure to meet commitments and the goods are not repossessed, the amount of bad debt is tantamount to extra income.

A third suspected source of exaggeration was the inclusion in the household budgets of expenditure on goods intended for resale.[2] Whereas the cost of these raw materials would normally be recovered in the course of business, the revenue from sales would not be reflected in the disclosed income of the household. The expenditure data obtained were analysed in an attempt to isolate these business costs but the results were inconclusive.[3] On the other hand, it might reasonably be supposed that households making large quantities of liquor would be reluctant to disclose any abnormally high purchases of raw material inputs.

A final factor which perhaps exaggerated expenditure was the trade in stolen goods. According to reports of fieldworkers, it was not uncommon for stolen goods of all kinds to be sold in these communities, and such goods changed hands at prices considerably lower than those in retail shops. Fieldworkers also reported that households which bought stolen goods often claimed to have paid the full retail price, even though the actual price paid may have been much lower. Three explanations for this behaviour may be suggested. First, informants might, for obvious reasons, have wished to conceal the fact that they were in possession of stolen goods; second, they might have had in mind the possibility of reselling the goods to the fieldworker; and third, the prevailing retail price of an expensive article (which had actually been bought very cheaply) might have been quoted for prestige reasons.

While one or more of these causes of exaggeration may have been present in many of the households, it is impossible that they could all have occurred in every household, and it is difficult to imagine how the consequent distortion of the mean expenditure could account for more than a part of the apparent discrepancy between disclosed wage income and actual expenditure.

It is conceivable that an individual household may normally spend more than it earns by way of wage income in a given period, either through the accumulation of debt or by drawing upon past savings. This study has found that there was an insignificant amount of credit buying of most PDL components. Little conclusive evidence, however, was elicited regarding the extent of savings accumulation in the community. Apart from the indebtedness incurred by hire-purchase transactions, there is a likelihood that the high level of expenditure compared with wage income may have been made possible through cash borrowing within a given period. A specific item in the survey schedule designed to obtain information on this aspect, however, elicited too meagre a response to enable the significance of this factor to be assessed. Just over one-half of the households reported indebtedness, and almost one-third had advanced cash loans to other individuals or households. The amounts were, however, not sufficiently large to explain the difference between the aggregate income and aggregate expenditure of the community.

Although questions were asked regarding the amounts of savings accumulated and their growth or diminution during the preceding year, the information obtained was of no assistance in establishing how much of past savings was being used to finance present expenditure. Relatively few informants could recall ever having surpluses or windfalls sufficient to form a nucleus of savings; only 16 per cent of the households declared any savings, the amounts generally being so small as to be safely ruled out as a significant factor in explaining the disparity between income and expenditure.

Thus, in the absence of any satisfactory explanation of the discrepancy either from exaggeration of expenditure by informants or from recourse to borrowings or accumulated reserves, attention must be turned to possible undisclosed sources of supplementary income.

SOURCES OF SUPPLEMENTARY INCOME

In an effort to ascertain the main informal sector activities which could explain the income deficit, a special investigation was undertaken among a sample of the households interviewed in the budget study.

Two areas within the Cato Manor Emergency Camp (Cabazini and Ezimbuzini) were selected. Cabazini was the heart of Cato Manor, consisting of flat land on the valley floor on either side of Booth Road. It contained the major bus stops, one of the largest unlicensed shack shops, a large Indian-owned trading store, and the Zulu *hlanganani sizanani* ('get together help each other') open market as well as many barbers and other informal services. Meat venders lined the road in the evening when the men returned from work and a large 'backyard' garage of 30–40 cars was strung along the road.

Initially the residents of Cabazini were co-operative but shortly after the inquiry commenced they were served with notices by the Durban Corporation warning them of their impending removal to KwaMashu. This resulted in hostility and lack of co-operation, which ultimately led to the transfer of fieldwork to Ezimbuzini, an area some 700 metres from Cabazini where removal notices had not yet been served. At Ezimbuzini, however, the atmosphere was tense since this area lay adjacent to KwaTickey[4] where the murder of nine policemen had taken place in January 1960; a number of Ezimbuzini residents were alleged to have been involved. As a result relatively few residents in this area co-operated. However, satisfactory co-operation from sufficient households in these areas of the Emergency Camp and in KwaMashu enabled us to reach a final sample of 100 households.[5]

Little co-operation was forthcoming from the residents of Lamont and Umlazi Glebe, largely because of the greater degree of political consciousness in these townships than in either Cato Manor or KwaMashu. There existed widespread suspicion that the disclosure of any type of personal information might prejudice leaders in these areas in the achievement of their political aspirations or, ultimately, that this evidence might be used to the detriment of individual respondents or of the community as a whole. However, group interviews were held and it was ascertained that residents in these areas experienced the difficulties common to all Africans in Durban and were forced to supplement their incomes wherever possible by means which they were reluctant to disclose except in general terms.

Various generally recognized means of supplementing income were adopted by people, sometimes singly or in combination, depending upon the opportunities which presented themselves. In general the use of these means was not regarded as morally defensible; rather, they were forced upon the community in order to 'make ends meet'. It was frequently emphasized that it was impossible for Africans to live in Durban if they were wholly dependent upon their disclosed earnings. A general increase in wages, it was contended, would prevent recourse to some of the methods being employed to supplement incomes.

It appeared that there were a number of socially acceptable ways in which households were able to supplement their incomes. Among the activities mentioned by women were knitting, dressmaking, cake-baking and the peddling of meat, vegetables and other goods.

When the budget survey was being carried out in 1959, several hundred labourers were employed in the construction of houses close to the sampling areas in KwaMashu. The initial absence of shops in the new township, and the fact that the municipal beerhall had not yet been opened and that police activities were negligible, enabled women to supplement household incomes by selling groceries to neighbours and beer and cooked food to construction workers. The growth in the number of shops, the movement of Corporation building-workers to sites further afield, the opening of a municipal beerhall, and the increased activities of the Municipal Security Corps subsequently changed the pattern of informal sector income. However, women could still be seen pushing prams loaded with cooked food and utensils to the distant areas where Corporation building-workers were engaged.

In the urban environment income from *lobolo*[6] was not very common and the community appeared to pay *lobolo* more frequently than it received it. *Stockfel*[7] hardly appeared at all as a source of income, although a few cases were noted in Cato Manor. *Maholisana*[8] was also rare but is, in any case, not a genuine source of income although it may affect a recipient household's expenditure pattern.

Although a number of households were engaged in various activities to supplement their earnings, the informants could seldom give a precise account of the revenue earned over any given period. These sources of income were, therefore, of little value for the purposes of this survey.

Our investigation isolated some of the major informal sources of income; these activities are typical of the informal sector in African cities[9] and are discussed below.

ILLICIT LIQUOR TRAFFIC

There can be little doubt that the proceeds from the manufacture and sale of illicit liquor accounted for a significant part of the undisclosed income of the African community of Durban. The only legal source of alcoholic beverages was the 'KB'[10] sold by municipal beerhalls, although householders could obtain permits to brew four gallons of beer per week at home for their own consumption.[11] However, the municipal beer had a low alcohol content and there was a ready demand for the stronger home-brewed beer,[12] for home-distilled spirits such as *gavine*[13] and for 'European' beers and spirits which sold at black-market prices;[14] these activities are described below. For obvious reasons, inquiries from individual households regarding the extent of their brewing and distilling activities, if any, and the revenue derived therefrom, proved abortive.

The main demand for illicit liquor in the urban area emanated largely from the concentrations of 'single' males[15] accommodated in barracks, hostels and compounds, and from those employed in private domestic service.[16] For the great majority of these people, the provision of liquor together with feminine company in the homely atmosphere of a *shebeen*[17] fulfilled a human need and constituted, in many cases, a necessary diversion in an otherwise humdrum existence.

Brewing and Sale of 'KB' and Shimeyane

Brewing formed the most important source of supplementary income for most households. It was almost exclusively in the hands of housewives. Prior to the riots in June 1959, the Durban Corporation exercised effective control of brewing activities through the issuing of permits to women brewing for family consumption.[18] After the riots, however, these regulations were relaxed, with the result that an increased number of women engaged in brewing for family consumption and for sale. Moreover, the temporary closing of the municipal beerhalls during and after the riots stimulated the demand for home-brewed beer and, in view of the considerable profits from the sale of beer, housewives became even more active in brewing.

Contrary to expectations, the reopening of the beerhalls after the riots did not result in a falling-off in the demand for home-brewed 'KB' and *shimeyane*, largely because of the higher alcohol content of these liquors. The beerhalls, after the riots, tended to become venues for social gatherings, suitable places for advertising, displaying and bartering stolen goods and for the activities of those who saw opportunities for making profits through the resale of municipal beer.[19]

The common practice was to use a 4-gallon tin for brewing purposes, while jam-tins (or 'scales') of three different sizes were used in measuring various quantities for sale.[20] Generally, between Thursdays and Sundays, which were the busy days, the housewife ensured that she had at least one tin (4 gallons) ready for sale every day. The contents of a 4-gallon tin of *shimeyane* usually fetched R1,25 and showed a net profit of 77 cents per tin while a similar quantity of 'KB', while also fetching R1,25, showed a net profit of only 55 cents per tin. [1 gallon = approx. 4,5 litres.]

The quantities and cost of the ingredients used in preparing these types of liquor accounted for the difference in net profit. The ingredients for producing a 4-gallon tin of *shimeyane* comprised 3 lb of malt, 2 lb of sugar, 2 loaves of brown bread and yeast, at a total cost of 48 cents, while the production of a similar quantity of 'KB' required 3 lb of mealie meal, 9 lb of malt and 1 lb of firewood, the total cost being 70 cents. [1 lb = approx. 450 grams.]

Distillation and Sale of Spirituous Liquors

During the 1950s the manufacture of *gavine* increased in importance as a source of supplementary income in the shack areas. But only a relatively small proportion of housewives engaged in its manufacture because of the comparatively long process of fermentation and distillation, the bulky apparatus required and the heavy fines imposed for being found in possession of the brew. Nevertheless, it constituted a lucrative source of supplementary income for those prepared to risk the consequences because of the considerable profits involved.

Gavine was usually prepared in 44-gallon drums, buried to their full depth in earth and covered by padlocked lids, while the ingredients (water, malt and sugar) went through the early stages of fermentation. After a fermentation period of five days, the product was distilled by the use of additional 44-gallon drums and an ingenious, if primitive, arrangement of enamel basins, after which the distillate was cooled and bottled. For the preparation of 44 gallons of undistilled *gavine* approximately 90 lb of brown sugar and 40 lb of malt (at a total estimated cost of R6) were required, together with fixed quantities of water. The distillate generally yielded 16 gallons of pure *gavine* or 96 bottles, which were sold to the *shebeens* in the area for 50 cents per bottle or were dispatched to Durban or farther afield and sold there at R1 per bottle. Transport costs and risks of police interference accounted largely for this difference in selling price.

Liquor Smuggling and the Sale of 'European' Liquor

At the time of the survey only a select group of Africans of good standing and possessing certain income and property ownership qualifications were entitled to apply to the native commissioners in the areas in which they resided for permits to possess and consume monthly certain specified quantities of 'European' liquor. This group was restricted mainly to professional persons, and to certain clerical and administrative staff in the municipal and government Bantu Administration departments. The liquor which they were allowed was purely for personal consumption and could not be supplied to relatives and friends.

These restrictions led to a considerable traffic in the townships in illicit 'European' liquor, which was almost as prevalent as brewing. Supplies were procured from Whites (usually at retail prices and involving no extra commission) or from Coloured suppliers (who were said to charge a commission of 50 cents per quart of spirits.) The retail price of cane spirit at the time was R1,20 and that of the cheapest brandies and other spirits R1,47½ per quart, but the selling prices at the *shebeens* and from individual resellers of liquor ranged from R2,40 in Cato Manor, Chesterville, Lamont and Umlazi Glebe, to R2,80 per quart in Clermont (near Pinetown) and KwaMashu. Supplies of illicit liquor from White sources at little above normal retail prices offered severe competition to '*shebeen* queens' and to women selling home-brewed or smuggled liquor acquired through Coloured suppliers, with the result that prices of spirits fell by one-fifth.

The consumption of 'European' liquor instead of 'KB' or *shimeyane* appeared to confer a superior social status. Thus even the average person who would normally drink only 'KB' or *shimeyane* tended to consume brandy and other 'European' spirits in addition.

HANDICRAFTS AND ARTISAN OCCUPATIONS

From time to time both men and women in these areas engaged in a number of craft activities as a source of supplementary income but the activities and the receipts therefrom were sporadic. Women did sewing and knitting while men undertook various skilled and semi-skilled tasks, mainly during week-ends. These included house-painting, repairs to furniture and mechanical equipment such as cars and scooters, and the installation of electrical appliances at Chesterville and Lamont. Scope for masons, carpenters and painters had been much wider during the growth of Cato Manor and particularly during the establishment of the Emergency Camp; such activities had declined with the implementation of the resettlement programme. Backyard mechanics were, however, found in all areas. Amongst the men, there was a tendency to regard earnings from these sources as personal 'pocket-money', the receipt of which was concealed from their families, with the result that income from these sources was not willingly disclosed.

MONEYLENDING, BORROWING AND USURY

When the original survey was undertaken there had been some reluctance on the part of informants to disclose detailed information which would enable the extent of borrowing and lending to be accurately assessed. This was due largely to the fact that such information was regarded as private and confidential in view of the stigma which was attached to the incurring of debts. Further inquiry, though no more successful than before in eliciting details of these transactions, served to confirm that borrowing and lending between individuals, and loans sought from moneylenders, were widespread. Moneylenders' loans, usually made over short periods ranging from a week to a month, often carried interest at the rate of 12 per cent per week or 50 per cent per month.

Loans were frequent and without loss of prestige between friends and neighbours when unforeseen emergencies arose and where sickness or death occurred in a household. The generally greater incidence of illness in the shack areas than in the established townships or in the White areas tended to increase the frequency of this type of borrowing. Frequent borrowing from persons within the community for purposes of meeting hire-purchase payments or commitments of a less urgent nature than illness or death involved a loss of prestige equally as grave as that of having goods repossessed through inability to maintain payment of instalments. Thus opportunities for cash borrowing were restricted by status considerations as well as by the limited sources and sizes of cash loans available in a largely indigent community. Consequently, when cash needs were urgent, expenditure on food and other essentials was reduced and when even this failed to relieve the pressure of perpetual debt, resort was eventually had to various illicit methods of supplementing income.

GAMBLING

Gambling on horse-races, at cards and *fahfee*[21] was common in the shack areas and established townships of Durban. However, the assessment of gains or losses over any specific period in order to determine the importance of gambling, either as a source of supplementary income or as an item of personal or household expenditure, proved impracticable.

SUNDRY ILLEGAL ACTIVITIES

Illegal activities such as theft, bribery and the buying and selling of stolen goods were common in this community. The amounts of income derived from these activities could not be obtained as residents clearly feared the consequences of any such disclosures.

Under the conditions of poverty existing in these areas it might have been expected that there would have been an appreciable market for prostitution. Although no suggestion of the existence of professional prostitution was made by fieldworkers, and authorities were unaware of any organized prostitution, it was known that this was an important source of income for some women. But it could not be expected that this aspect should be made a matter of inquiry in a survey of this nature, and there was thus no possibility of assessing its economic importance.

A further source of illegal income which might have been expected to contribute to the earnings of some households was the sale of *dagga* (marihuana). However, it proved impossible to establish the extent and regularity of supplementary income from this source.

Unlicensed general dealers and petty traders were common in Cato Manor, particularly in the uncontrolled shack areas where there were in 1958 some 55 well-established trading stores, i.e. with at least one room of a shack devoted to the storage of stocks and the conducting of business. In the Emergency Camp a tighter control was exercised on trading activities, but despite the existence of licensed shops (usually operated by ex-illegal traders) some unlicensed trade was conducted. As in the case of other unlicensed trading activities such as repair shops and secondhand-car dealers which have already been mentioned, no income figures were disclosed. Pirate taxi operators were not as common as might have been expected in Cato Manor in view of the numerous car repairers and dealers. The reason was that the area was well served by African-owned, Indian-owned and municipal bus services.

Apart from these informal sector sources of supplementary income, further (legal) sources which were identified were the receipt of gratuities from employers and assistance from relatives. Gratuities received from White employers were treated as private 'pocket-money' in the same manner as the proceeds from handicrafts. These amounts, however, were seldom disclosed and thus did not figure as part of the household income. Further inquiries into gratuities as a source of supplementary income confirmed the expectation that they were occasional and relatively insignificant in amount.

Similarly, assistance received from relatives in cash and in kind appeared to be both irregular and of minor significance. Though a few families indicated that they were regularly in receipt of support from relatives, the majority turned to relatives for help only in emergencies. The dearth of specific information regarding the provision of food-stuffs, clothing, etc., by relatives within the urban areas as well as by those in the Reserves precluded a reliable estimate being made of the frequency and value of these contributions to household maintenance.

THE STATE OF PERPETUAL INDEBTEDNESS

The majority of African householders in Durban were in what may be termed a 'state of perpetual indebtedness' as a result of the inability of their incomes to encompass their minimum requirements in the urban environment. This invariably led to comparisons being made with the affluent standards of the White community. A view frequently expressed was that under the modernizing influence of the urban areas, African families were fast adopting White tastes and habits. Moreover, certain commodities considered as unnecessary 'European' luxuries by the preceding generation had, in fact, become necessities for the present one, so that the needs of the average African family had broadened in range and advanced in quality as a result of urban residence. Prices of most of these needs, it was contended, were geared to the White community's requirements and standards which either put them beyond the reach of the low-income group or demanded the expenditure of a major proportion of the total income of this group.[22] In order, therefore, to procure these commodities which had become necessities in the urban environment, the lower income groups were inevitably obliged to incur debt or seek to supplement their incomes by engaging in practices which were not countenanced by the Westernized society in which economic necessity had obliged them to live.

It may be assumed that the production and eventual exchange of goods and services within a community add to its income. But the lack of a secondary, followed by a tertiary increase, and so on, and the magnitude of leakages when additional income is spent on items which cannot be procured locally, weaken the multiplier effect. Yet, since the community is not a closed one, a significant amount of goods and services may be sold to customers from outside, thus creating an important source of undisclosed income. Thus, whether this undisclosed income arises from legal or illegal sources, and whether it can be morally justified or not, there can be no question that it performs an important economic function by bolstering the community's standard of living. This conclusion is substantiated by the views of the ILO (quoted on p. 4) that in a poor community the informal sector provides a wide range of essential goods and services.

APPENDIX TO CHAPTER 3

A SELECTION OF RESPONSES TO INQUIRIES DESIGNED TO DETERMINE REASONS FOR THE DISCREPANCY BETWEEN DISCLOSED INCOME AND HOUSEHOLD EXPENDITURE

Q1. *Can you account for the discrepancy which exists between your disclosed earnings and your household expenditure?*
    1. The difference may be due to the few shillings I get from selling beer and cooked food.
    2. It may have resulted from brewing, the use of savings or from borrowing.

3. There are a number of things which may have caused the difference.
4. I am not quite sure. Maybe it comes naturally, on its own.
5. I have savings in the Post Office.
6. Maybe I have saved in the previous week though it is not shown on your schedule.
7. All the time I have not been aware that there is this difference so I cannot account for it.
8. It is very difficult to explain this difference since I do not keep records of my expenditures.
9. You told me of the difference. I think you are in a better position, too, to tell me how it arises.
10. What do you mean? Are you implying that the information I gave you is false?
11. In order to give you a good answer, I shall have to think for a considerable time.
12. This is a difficult question. I cannot give a straightforward answer.

Q2. *Is it possible for you to raise funds elsewhere to supplement your earnings?*

1. What was once possible has been made impossible by the 'Black Jacks'.[1]
2. I have got savings and my wife brews 'KB'.
3. If you are badly in need it is always possible to raise some few shillings here and there.
4. At times I collect a few shillings when I sell beer.
5. Do you think I can support the family with only £3.15.0 [R7,50] a week?
6. Do you think that I can depend solely on this weekly income which is so little that it is as good as not there?
7. As an African[2] you should know that we cannot live on our disclosed income.
8. How do you think I can support myself and my family if I do not supplement my income?
9. Are you seriously suggesting that an African can live in Durban without using his wits to supplement his income?
10. Do you think I am so foolish as to remain in Durban and not supplement my income?
11. Because of low wages, the Africans are forced to commit a number of crimes and offences in order to supplement their incomes.
12. In order to remain at KwaMashu, I must keep on supplementing my income.

[1] Durban Bantu Administration Department's Security Corps.
[2] These interviews were carried out by an African graduate.

Q3. *Can you indicate the nature and sources of your undisclosed supplementary income?*

1. Last year I ran an unlicensed general dealer's shop, but that has now been stopped and I depend on brewing for extra money.
2. I have savings in the Post Office and I occasionally sell European liquor.
3. My wife is a part-time washerwoman and I repair furniture for my neighbours during my spare time.
4. My wife brews and I use my wits to supplement my income.
5. I am a bricklayer. On Saturdays, when I am not working, a number of people employ me to improve their houses (plastering and painting) for which they pay me.
6. If my car is in good condition, I carry people to different places, for which they pay me. I get tips and otherwise use my wits to obtain money.
7. I hope you will be honest with me and not reveal this information to the police. The sources of my additional income are: smuggled liquor, gambling and other illegal activities.
8. As I am of Coloured descent I am able to obtain liquor from bottlestores and sell it.
9. I use my wits and get money in a number of illegal ways which I am not prepared to tell you.
10. Borrowing, traffic in smuggled liquor, gambling and other illicit means of getting money.
11. Borrowing, brewing, traffic in illicit liquor and support from relatives.
12. I have been selling food and 'KB' to labourers but the Corporation has tightened up its regulations now and the 'Black Jacks' raid us often.

Q4. *Is supplementary income from these sources regularly or spasmodically received?*

1. How do you expect me to live if I do not do these things regularly?
2. I am in debt even now as we are speaking. Please just buy my liquor. I shall give you a quart of beer for 5s. because I know you.
3. Income from washing is fairly regular but carpentry work is available only occasionally.
4. It is difficult to say categorically whether I do these things regularly but brewing takes place almost every week-end. I am always having minor debts and in using my wits, I depend on chance.

5. There is usually work for me to do at week-ends.
6. Not regularly—whenever I get a chance.
7. Whether it is regular or irregular, that is immaterial. It all depends on chance and my need of money at that moment.
8. I think I can say it is a regular source of supplementary income.
9. I cannot say whether it is regular or not, but whenever I get a chance I make good use of it.
10. I literally live on this supplementary income.
11. I am in debt even at this moment. I brew beer every day and sell smuggled liquor every week-end. My son-in-law sends his children money at the rate of about £3 per month.
12. I used to sell food every day, but now as they are working in a further area I have become lazy to carry food to them every day.

Q5. *What proportion of your regular weekly/monthly earnings does this supplementary income form?*

1. Sometimes it is more, sometimes less than my wages.
2. It is less, far less, than income from wages.
3. It was pounds and pounds less.
4. Though it is less, it makes such a difference to my expenses.
5. Whenever I am in difficulties I withdraw savings.
6. I cannot be definite. It all depends on chance and luck.
7. At times it was more.
8. All I know is that it is a supplementary income. Whether it is more or less than my wages is immaterial. I have never compared it with my earnings.
9. It is usually two or three times as much as my earnings.
10. That is a childish question. You are well aware of the fact that I get this money to spend it then and there. I never record it so I do not know.
11. Last year it used to be more. These days the 'Black Jacks' are barring my way.
12. Last year I was really making money. It was always either almost the same or more than my wages.

Q6. *Does supplementary income from undisclosed sources make up the difference between your disclosed earnings and your expenditure?*

1. It amounts to that.
2. That is the only way one can account for this difference.
3. I am sure that this additional income, though less, is the main factor which has brought about this difference.
4. Yes. That is the factor which I can say accounts for this difference you are talking about.

5. Yes, that is true because occasional outside work and withdrawals of savings are the only sources of supplementary income I have.
6. I think you will not be far wrong in understanding that.
7. I think it is just like that.
8. You will not be far wrong in that conclusion.
9. What else can you understand except that?
10. That is obvious. Please do not waste my time!
11. Yes, you are right, I think the income from these sources accounts for the difference.
12. It is very likely that selling food and brewing causes the difference.

NOTES AND REFERENCES

1 Barber, op. cit., pp. 116–17.
2 Materials used in beer-brewing or in the preparation of meals for sale would be included here.
3 Largely because of the difficulty in distinguishing between those materials (particularly items such as mealie-meal, sugar, paraffin, etc.) which were bought for actual personal consumption by household members, and those used for 'manufacturing' purposes or resale.
4 A shed in which milk was sold for threepence ('tickey') a pint and into which the policemen had retreated.
5 A selected sample of the responses given appears in the Appendix to the chapter.
6 'Bride-price' paid to the wife's parents, traditionally to compensate for the loss of progeny.
7 A private gathering at which food and drink are sold or auctioned to raise money for the host, the role of host circulating among members of the participating group.
8 A system whereby a group of people agree to pool contributions every week, the total amount being given to each member in rotation.
9 For a discussion of similar activities in another South African city (East London) see: Philip Mayer, *Townsmen or Tribesmen*, Cape Town: Oxford University Press, 1961, pp. 140 and 247.
10 This is derived from the old term 'Kaffir beer' which is no longer acceptable. The official term, 'Bantu beer', is also unacceptable to township dwellers who commonly refer to the beer as 'KB'. The traditionalists refer to it as 'utshwala besizulu', i.e. Zulu beer, while it is also sometimes known as 'mgombothi'.
11 In terms of Government Notice No. 88 of 21 January 1949 the municipal authority was empowered to issue permits valid for 7–28 days which allowed householders to brew from 2–10 gallons per week, solely for the consumption of the householder and his immediate family. During 1958–9 some 3 000 permits per week were issued to residents of Cato Manor. Approximately 75 per cent of the households at KwaMashu, 50 per cent at Lamont and 75 per cent at Umlazi Glebe regularly applied for brewing permits in these years.
12 According to official evidence, presented to the Supreme Court, Durban in August 1960, a quantity of 123 000 gallons of illicit *shimeyane* (unfermented liquor) was destroyed by the police over a period of ten days during the course of liquor raids on Cato Manor.
13 In June 1959, during the demolition of Tintown, a shack area adjacent to the Cato Manor Emergency Camp which housed 232 African families, some 25 liquor

stills for the manufacture of *gavine* were uncovered. A single brew from each still produced approximately 12 bottles of *gavine* which sold for R1 per bottle.

14 It was only three years later—on 14 August 1962— that the purchase of 'European' liquor by Africans was legalized.

15 Unmarried men as well as married migrant male labourers whose families were still resident in the Reserves.

16 In 1960 approximately 26 500 single African males were accommodated in municipal hostels and barracks and in Railway, government and private compounds. An estimated further 62 500 persons, both male and female, were housed in licensed premises and as domestic servants on residential premises.

17 A bar lounge-cum-nightclub in a private dwelling presided over by a '*shebeen* queen'.

18 A source of dissatisfaction with these regulations, it was alleged, arose from the fact that the police apparently interpreted the phrase 'for family consumption' as applying only to the head of the household and his wife, so that other members of the family, e.g. the sons, were not covered by the permit and were liable to be arrested if found drinking with their parents.

19 The procedure customarily adopted was to purchase quantities of beer, keep it until the beerhalls' supplies were exhausted and thereafter sell it to latecomers at a profit. Quantities costing 20 cents at beerhall prices were usually sold for 40 cents in these transactions.

20 The contents of a 2 lb jam-tin ($1\frac{1}{4}$ pints) were sold for 5 cents, that of a 4 lb tin ($2\frac{1}{2}$ pints) for 10 cents and that of an 8 lb tin (5 pints) for 20 cents.

21 A kind of privately organized lottery in which the stakes are usually very low.

22 An example frequently quoted was a White with a monthly income of R200 who bought in the same market and at the same prices as an African earning R24 per month.

PART II

BEYOND CATO MANOR

by

GAVIN MAASDORP and P. A. ELLISON

CHAPTER 4

Resettlement

We have already discussed African housing conditions in Durban (chapter 1) and the economic position of households (Part I) during the late 1950s. This chapter records developments in the housing of the African community since 1957, one year before resettlement began.

THE END OF CATO MANOR

The Cato Manor Emergency Camp was opened in 1952. When fully developed it consisted of 4 427 sites, each structure containing four rooms and a kitchen.[1] In many shacks the kitchens were, however, used for living purposes, cooking being done either in the open or in the living-rooms. Each shack housed an estimated 4–5 families and in its heyday the population of the camp was probably about 90 000. This figure included a large number of boarders. Population estimates for Cato Manor itself varied, but at its peak the area probably contained some 120 000 inhabitants and was one of the worst slums in South Africa.

The removal programme commenced in March 1958, and was almost complete by August 1965. By this date 6 062 shacks in Cato Manor had been cleared; 18 307 families and 2 251 single males, making a total of 82 826 persons, had officially been resettled in the new townships of KwaMashu and Umlazi. But only those families which had permits to be in Durban were rehoused, and it appears that some 30 000–40 000 persons must have 'disappeared' during the programme, either returning to their rural areas or else taking up illegal residence elsewhere in the city; some infiltrated into other areas of Cato Manor to gain what could only be a temporary respite.

There is plenty of evidence of the extent of illegal presence in Durban, quite apart from pass-book offences. In the Thusini area of Cato Manor, for example, only 368 of 855 families were found to be eligible to remain in Durban. At Ezinkaweni, Mnyasana and Emhlangeni, 56 per cent of the families disappeared during clearance operations. In 1961 it was stated that of the 4 722 families which had been moved from the uncontrolled areas of Cato Manor, 2 522 had been resettled in KwaMashu, 1 587 in the Emergency Camp and 613 (or 13 per cent) had disappeared in transit.

The Cato Manor Emergency Camp represented a relatively orderly arrangement, and the resultant thinning out of the uncontrolled shack areas on the periphery of the camp simplified to some extent the formidable task of resettlement. It soon became clear that the uncontrolled areas should be eliminated before any substantial removals from the camp were initiated.

Thus the first area to be cleared was 'Raincoat', the most notorious of the slum areas. After a preliminary survey the population was estimated at 4 000, but clearance operations revealed a figure of 5 900 persons living in the 248 shacks in the area, i.e. almost 24 persons per shack. These shacks contained a total of 1 682 rooms, giving an occupancy rate of 3,5 persons per room. The Raincoat residents were resettled either in KwaMashu, where the first houses were occupied in March 1958, or in the Emergency Camp. Raincoat was cleared by August 1958, and work then started at Thusini (Haviland Road). Conditions were somewhat less crowded than at Raincoat, the same number of shacks (248) housing 3 350 persons, or 13 per shack.

During the early stages of the removal programme considerable resistance was encountered from the inhabitants. Apart from the large number of illegal residents who saw the move as depriving them of any abode in Durban, the illegal operators in the informal sector—the racketeers, thieves,[2] 'shebeen queens', etc.—saw their livelihood threatened. Moreover, there was concern at the prospect of increased living costs in the new townships because of higher rentals and transport expenses.

This resistance first manifested itself in April 1959 when demonstrations against the demolition of shacks at Mnyasana caused the programme to be halted. Then in June 1959 there was a spontaneous protest which led to the destruction of buildings and facilities in the Emergency Camp. Following a slight typhoid epidemic steps were taken to clear up insanitary conditions within the camp; this involved the destruction of open drums of illicit liquor found buried in vacant ground. Demonstrations were held against the sale of 'KB' at the municipal beerhall and a sustained boycott, symbolic of the state of unrest among the African community of the city, commenced.[3] The removal programme was halted during this period but was resumed in November 1959 under police protection.

Further unrest occurred during the first four months of 1960. In January a routine liquor raid in Cato Manor involving the destruction of liquor stills resulted in the murder of nine policemen (five of them African). At the end of March, after the violence at Sharpeville and Langa, some 6 000 Africans marched from Cato Manor to the city centre to demand the release of their arrested leaders. The Emergency Camp was surrounded by police and army units, and conditions were soon back to normal. After these incidents resistance to the removals tended to disappear.

By the end of 1959 Raincoat, Thusini, Dunbar Road and Tintown had been cleared, and some 10 600 persons had been resettled. But from 1960 to 1964 the pace of removals increased. During the first eight months of 1960 alone 17 700 persons were resettled and fifteen areas were cleared.[4] At that stage all the uncontrolled areas outside the Emergency Camp had been cleared and the only shack areas remaining were the Emergency Camp itself and the African-owned areas of Chateau Estate, Good Hope Estate[5] and Matatiele.

In November 1960, after several notices to residents, the elimination of shacks in the Emergency Camp began. It was preceded, once again, by the expression of considerable concern by the residents at the prospect of the increased rent and transport costs that they would have to meet at KwaMashu. Early in 1961, however, it appeared that there had been a change of attitude by the residents and about 400–500 families per month were asking to be moved to the KwaMashu housing scheme. The official explanation of this change was that the residents realized that they would be leaving the squalor and overcrowding of Durban's worst slum area, but a more likely explanation is that they realized the inevitability of resettlement and thus attempted to get into the queue for new housing as soon as possible. Moreover, occupation of a municipal house would end any insecurity they might have felt about their right to reside in the urban area.

During 1961 twelve areas of the Emergency Camp were eliminated.[6] In 1962 removals slowed down because of building delays at Kwa-Mashu, but nevertheless Two Sticks, Mjafete, KwaBhengu, Newlook and KwaMnguni were cleared. This was followed in 1963 by Mount Carmel, Kumalo and Dabulamanzi. In the meantime the first houses at Umlazi became available in May 1962 for residents of Cato Manor and KwaMashu who were employed in the southern part of the city—165 families from Cato Manor and 96 from KwaMashu were resettled there—and by 1963 Umlazi was absorbing 50 per cent of those removed from Cato Manor.

At the end of July 1963, 1 113 shacks containing an estimated 18 700 persons remained in the Emergency Camp. The camp was finally cleared on 31 August 1964 and thereafter attention was devoted to eliminating the remaining shack areas of Chateau and Good Hope Estates and Matatiele. Together these areas contained 434 shacks and a population of 6 400. During the following twelve months 983 families were moved and by August 1966 only nine shacks remained in the Cato Manor area.

Today the hillsides of Cato Manor are once again covered by thick tropical bush and grass. A few paved roads, shells of buildings burnt in the 1959 riots and traffic to and from Chesterville are the sole reminders of human settlement. Some Indian families who have thus far survived the Group Areas axe still live on the periphery. Cato Manor today represents one of the largest undeveloped urban areas in a South African city and is soon to be developed as a housing estate for 17 000 White families.

OTHER AREAS

Cato Manor was not the only African area cleared in terms of the Group Areas Act. Other shack areas in Durban were also eliminated, the last clearance (the small pocket at Happy Valley on the Bluff)[7] being effected in 1967. It appears from official records that some 640 shacks in these areas, housing at least 10 000 persons, were demolished. If this figure is added to the 82 000 who had been moved from Cato Manor by 1965 (page 61) and those moved in 1966, it would seem that approximately 95 000 Africans were resettled from the shack areas of Durban.

But it was not only the shack areas which disappeared. Baumannville, the city's oldest African township, was declared a non-residential area and was all but cleared by the end of 1959, finally being deproclaimed as an African area in 1962. The barracks at Bell Street and Ordnance Road, containing 1 165 and 440 single males respectively, were evacuated in 1959 and the men rehoused in a hostel in KwaMashu. The Somtseu Road hostel, containing 7 040 beds, was closed in 1962. Thus from Baumannville and the hostels a further 9 450 persons were removed. Not all of these settled in KwaMashu; for example, of those moved from Somtseu Road in 1961 only 50 per cent went to Kwa-Mashu and the place of abode of the rest was a 'mystery'.[8]

PRESENT ACCOMMODATION

Durban's African population today resides in accommodation ranging from family houses to compounds or hostels and 'kias' (for domestic servants). This accommodation has been provided by the local authority, the state and employers, but in August 1973 there was a change in the administration of African townships in Durban and the Corporation is no longer directly involved in African township affairs. The following discussion is primarily concerned with the situation obtaining before the takeover while the present position is referred to briefly in chapter 5.

Table 4.1 shows the number of family housing units available in the Durban municipal townships and Umlazi since 1957.[9] In the smaller townships, there has been an increase of 604 houses in Lamont and a loss of 854 houses in Umlazi Glebe and Baumannville, resulting in an overall net loss of 250 houses since 1957. But for all the townships together there was a net addition of 33 360 houses in the period 1957–70. The planning and construction of housing in the townships were undertaken by the Durban Corporation. The Corporation also administered all the townships except Umlazi, which fell under the central government (the Department of Bantu Administration and Development); however, the Corporation undertook the planning and construction of Umlazi as the agent of the South African Bantu Trust.

Accommodation in family units in Durban and Umlazi is analysed in Table 4.2. The population figures are estimates, but there is every

Aerial view of part of Cato Manor, 1961, showing terracing on hillside (towards top left centre) and school (centre of foreground).

(Photo: Natal Mercury)

Cato Manor beerhall with shacks in background, 1959.

(Photo: Natal Mercury)

Shumville, Cato Manor, showing dwellings erected with the aid of a Corporation loan for building materials.

(Photo: Colin Shum)

Cabazini, Cato Manor, showing controlled L-shaped dwellings.
(Photo: Colin Shum)

Cato Manor, 1964, showing one of the last areas to be cleared.

Scene at the Zulu *hlanganani sizanani* market, Cato Manor.

The beginnings of KwaMashu, 1959, showing its location amidst the cane fields.
(Photo: Natal Mercury)

Aerial view of section of KwaMashu, 1974, showing suburban railway line and main road (bisecting photograph in the centre), neighbourhood units, sportsfields and schools.

(*Photo*: Land Surveying Department, University of Natal)

Queue at the Victoria Street bus rank, Durban.

(*Photo*: Moosa Badsha, *The Graphic*)

Township residents waiting for a train at Berea Road Station, Durban.

(*Photo*: Moosa Badsha, *The Graphic*)

New hostel for single men at Clermont near Pinetown.

(*Photo:* Moosa Badsha, *The Graphic*)

New squatter area at Clermont near Pinetown.

(*Photo:* Moosa Badsha, *The Graphic*)

Table 4.1

DISTRIBUTION OF TOTAL NUMBER OF FAMILY HOUSES IN DURBAN AND UMLAZI,
1957–70

As at 31 July	Lamont and Extension	Chester-ville	Baumann-ville	Umlazi Glebe	Kwa-Mashu[a]	Umlazi [b]	Total
1957	2 158[c]	1 265	120	734	–	–	4 277
1958	2 700	1 265	120	734	384	–	5 203
1959	2 709	1 265	60	735	1 595	–	6 364
1960	2 717	1 265	60	735	5 115	–	9 892
1961	2 727	1 265	60	732	8 788	–	13 572
1962	2 744	1 265	–	746	10 405	1 255	16 415
1963	2 760	1 265	–	748	11 517	3 342	19 632
1964	2 762	1 265	–	748	12 502	7 368	24 645
1965	2 762	1 265	–	748	14 059[d]	9 482	28 316
1966	2 762	1 265	–	748	13 144	11 205	29 124
1967	2 762	1 265	–	425	13 914	14 458	32 824
1968	2 762	1 265	–	–	14 072	15 945	34 044
1969	2 762	1 265	–	–	14 742	17 351	36 120
1970	2 762	1 265	–	–	15 256	18 254	37 537

Notes: (a) These figures exclude houses built for single accommodation.

(b) From 1964, 1 123 of these houses have been used temporarily as single accommodation. It is planned to provide single accommodation on a portion of land between the Isipingo and Umbogintwini rivers.

(c) The Lamont Extension economic housing scheme, started in 1956, was almost complete in 1958; the small additions in subsequent years finally totalled 851 houses in 1964.

(d) The discrepancy in this figure is possibly due to a clerical error in the assessment of temporary huts.

reason to believe that they err on the conservative side.[10] The table includes the controlled accommodation in the Cato Manor Emergency Camp which was completely evacuated in August 1964. In 1957, permanent family housing, excluding the camp, provided accommodation for only 28 000 persons. The provision by 1970 of permanent family housing for an additional 227 000 Africans in fully serviced residential areas is a noteworthy achievement.

Table 4.3 shows the provision of permanent accommodation for single people by the Durban Corporation.[11] Accommodation for single women has been constant and limited. It is government policy to restrict urban entry permits to women as it considers that there is a sufficient number living in the Durban area to satisfy all employment needs. In October 1968 the entry to Durban of African female domestic servants from the Transkei was forbidden, and in January 1969 requisitioning from other parts of South Africa was discontinued. However, there seems to be considerable pressure on the available accommodation and an attempt is being made to provide some accommodation for women at KwaMashu. The difficulty seems to be the high cost of the

Table 4.2

DISTRIBUTION OF POPULATION IN FAMILY ACCOMMODATION IN DURBAN AND UMLAZI, 1957–70

As at 31 July	Lamont and Extension	Chester-ville	Baumann-ville	Umlazi Glebe	Cato Manor (a)	Kwa-Mashu	Umlazi (b)	Total
1957	14 500	8 000	800	4 700	35 000	–	–	63 000
1958	18 400	7 600	800	4 700	40 000	2 000	–	73 500
1959	18 500	7 900	46	5 100	46 500	10 000	–	88 000
1960	18 500	7 900	46	5 100	55 500	25 000	–	112 000
1961	17 400	8 000	–	4 600	40 000	43 000	–	113 000
1962	16 500	7 600	–	4 500	35 000	55 700	8 800	128 100
1963	17 000	8 000	–	4 500	20 000	66 700	23 400	139 600
1964	19 000	8 900	–	4 600	2 200	80 000	43 700	158 400
1965	20 700	9 300	–	5 000	–	88 200	58 600	181 800
1966	20 700	9 300	–	5 000	–	90 600	70 600	196 200
1967	20 700	9 300	–	3 000	–	94 000	93 400	220 400
1968	20 700	9 300	–	–	–	95 000	103 800	228 800
1969	20 700	9 300	–	–	–	102 000	113 700	245 700
1970	20 800	9 300	–	–	–	106 000	120 000	256 100

Notes: (a) Cato Manor Emergency Camp.

(b) Excluding family houses being used for single accommodation.

type of accommodation envisaged. This may be a reason, too, for the delay in increasing the single accommodation for men at Umlazi Glebe.

In 1961, there was a large build-up of beds in KwaMashu in anticipation of the closing of the Somtseu Road Location. The Africans, however, regarded the cottage type of accommodation (four persons to each unit) with some misgivings, and for a few years there was a considerable number of vacant beds, at one time as many as 4 000. However, there were few vacant beds after 1963.

Table 4.4 shows the accommodation of Durban's African population not included in the previous two tables (it does, however, exclude the Cato Manor Emergency Camp). The figures relate only to official numbers which means the number disclosed or that could be counted. The total of 68 300 represents less than one-fifth of the African population of Durban and Umlazi. Some of those living on licensed premises are provided with family accommodation, but even if the figure in this category is halved, it is evident that there would have to be an extensive programme of single accommodation in African residential areas to house those single persons at present living in state and private accommodation in Durban.

The figures for shacks relate mainly to the periphery of the Emergency Camp. Accommodation on African-owned property in the Cato Manor

Table 4.3

DISTRIBUTION OF POPULATION IN MUNICIPAL SINGLE ACCOMMODATION IN DURBAN, 1957–70

As at 31 July	Males							Females			Total
	Hostels (a) built prior to 1962 and other	Dalton Road Location	Jacobs Hostel	S.J. Smith Hostel	KwaMashu	Umlazi Glebe Hostel	Total	Jacobs Hostel	Grey St. Hostel	Total	Total
1957	9 632	1 662	788	4 272	—	—	16 354	64	687	751	17 105
1958	9 645	1 662	788	4 272	—	—	16 367	64	687	751	17 118
1959	9 645	1 662	788	4 272	—	—	16 367	64	687	751	17 118
1960	8 040	1 662	788	4 272	3 168	—	17 930	64	687	751	18 681
1961	8 040	1 662	788	4 592	8 000	—	23 082(c)	64	687	751	23 833
1962	1 200	1 662	788	4 602	10 224	—	18 476	64	687	751	19 227
1963	1 200	1 662	828	4 602	11 312	—	19 604	32	687	719	20 323
1964	1 200	1 721	828	4 602	12 240	—	20 591	32	687	719	21 310
1965	1 200	1 721	828	4 602	13 008	—	21 359	32	687	719	22 078
1966	1 000	1 451(b)	828	4 602	14 160	—	22 041	32	687	719	22 760
1967	600	1 450	841	4 652	15 936	1 289	24 768	14	687	698	25 466
1968	600	1 450	886	4 481	16 880	2 900	27 197	—	684	684	27 831
1969	600	1 450	886	4 481	16 880	2 993	27 290	—	684	684	27 974
1970	600	1 450	886	4 481	17 650	3 012	28 079	—	677	677	28 756

Notes: (a) By 1960 both the Ordance Road Location and Bell Street Hostel with accommodation for 1 165 and 440 persons respectively were closed. Somtseu Road Location with accommodation for 7 040 persons was closed in 1962. The balance refers mainly to accommodation for municipal emergency gangs.

(b) Dalton Road Location lost a large portion of one building due to the widening of Sydney Road.

(c) There were, in addition, 200 members of the Security Corps housed temporarily at Baumannville.

Table 4.4

DISTRIBUTION OF STATE AND PRIVATE SINGLE ACCOMMODATION IN DURBAN[a] AND
UMLAZI, 1957–70

As at 31 July	Railway and Government compounds	Licensed premises	Domestic servants	African-owned property	Shacks	Umlazi (state)	Total
1957	8 000	29 500	30 000	500	22 000	–	90 000
1958	8 000	29 500	30 000	500	32 000	–	100 000
1959	8 000	30 000	31 500	500	31 500	–	101 500
1960	8 000	31 000	31 500	1 000	8 500	–	80 000
1961	8 000	32 000	31 500	4 800	1 800	–	78 100
1962	8 000	32 000	31 500	4 500	2 500	–	78 500
1963	8 000	32 000	31 500	6 500	2 500	–	80 500
1964	7 300	25 200	31 500	6 500	2 500	7 861	80 861
1965	7 300	25 200	31 500	1 100	4 500	7 861	77 461
1966	7 000	24 500	31 500	250	150	7 861	71 261
1967	6 400	24 300	31 500	200	–	7 861	70 261
1968	6 400	24 300	31 500	200	–	7 861	70 261
1969	6 400	24 000	30 000	–	–	7 861	68 261
1970	6 400	24 000	30 000	–	–	7 861	68 261

Note: (a) Excluding the Cato Manor Emergency Camp.

area appears to have been inversely related to the shack population
before it was acquired by the Durban Corporation and private buyers.

The reduced accommodation in Railway and government compounds was due to the closure in stages of the Greyville compound.
The decrease in the number living on licensed premises resulted from
the application of the Bantu Laws Amendment Act No. 76 of 1963,
the object of which was to remove apartment and hotel workers to
the townships.[12] There is little variation in the number of Durban's
domestic servants living on premises owned by Whites. The government brake on the introduction of females into the area has probably
been accompanied, over the years, by an increase in the number of
domestic servants who commute daily from the townships.

HOUSING AND POPULATION GROWTH

Any progress in the elimination of slums and in the provision of mass
low-cost housing must be weighed against housing requirements
arising from continued population growth. Hance has pinpointed
the dilemma which faces urban housing authorities in Africa: '... the
more attention given to the city the more attractive it becomes and
hence the greater the migration to it is likely to be, thus perpetuating
if not heightening the problem.'[13]

Table 4.5 collates the figures in the three preceding tables to show the
total accommodation available in Durban and Umlazi, thus indicating the total disclosed African population. However, some of the

Table 4.5

DISTRIBUTION OF AFRICAN POPULATION BY TYPE OF ACCOMMODATION IN DURBAN
AND UMLAZI, 1957–70

As at 31 July	Durban				Umlazi (all state)			Total
	Family (municipal)	Single	Single (state and private)	Total	Family	Single	Total	
1957	63 000	17 105	90 000	170 105	–	–	–	170 105
1958	73 500	17 118	100 000	190 618	–	–	–	190 618
1959	88 000	17 118	101 500	206 618	–	–	–	206 618
1960	112 000	18 681	80 000	210 681	–	–	–	210 681
1961	113 000	23 833	78 100	214 933	–	–	–	214 933
1962	119 300	19 227	78 500	217 027	8 800	–	8 800	225 827
1963	116 200	20 323	80 500	217 023	23 400	–	23 400	240 423
1964	114 700	21 310	73 000	209 010	43 700	7 861	51 561	260 571
1965	123 200	22 078	69 600	214 878	58 600	7 861	66 461	281 339
1966	125 600	22 760	63 400	211 760	70 600	7 861	78 461	290 221
1967	127 000	25 466	62 400	214 866	93 400	7 861	101 261	316 127
1968	125 000	27 881	62 400	215 281	103 800	7 861	111 661	326 942
1969	132 000	27 974	60 400	220 374	113 700	7 861	121 561	341 935
1970	136 100	28 756	60 400	225 256	120 000	7 861	127 861	353 117

figures are mere assessments, and the total of 353 000 is slightly higher than that revealed by the 1970 population census for Durban and Umlazi, viz. 328 000. The figure of 395 000 in Table 1.2 relates to the entire metropolitan area, which includes the townships in the Pinetown area such as Clermont, Klaarwater and Mariannhill.

According to census figures (Table 1.2) the African population of the DMA increased from 222 000 to 395 000 in the inter-censal period 1960–70. This represents an average annual rate of increase of 6,2 per cent, which is considerably higher than the rate of 5 per cent calculated by Young for Durban and Umlazi for the period 1960–4,[14] or the national figure of 3,4 per cent for Africans from 1960 to 1970. Moreover, in evaluating population census data, Sadie found that the latter figure should have been no more than 2,65 per cent.[15] The rate of 6,2 per cent should be treated with caution in view of the inaccuracy of census counts. Bearing in mind that recent studies indicate a falling size of African families in urban areas due to the adoption of birth-control practices, it is clear that this figure is well over double that of the rate of natural increase, thus implying a high rate of net migration from the rural areas.

It appears that this migration was most rapid after 1964. The average number of African males in registered employment in Durban increased from 120 000 in July 1959 to 124 700 in July 1964; this was followed by a rapid increase to 139 100 in July 1965 and 151 400 in

July 1967. During the following year these numbers declined to 147 800 due to the introduction of new legislation requiring those who ceased to be employed from April 1968 to register with the labour bureau in their home district. But thereafter the numbers increased again to 150 200 in July 1970 and 158 500 two years later.[16] However, officials readily admit that there are large numbers of Africans working in Durban without the necessary permits, so that even these figures provide only a rough idea of the position.

We have already referred, in chapter 1, to census underenumeration of urban African populations. Tables 1.2, 4.2 and 4.5 are based on official figures and must be regarded as highly inaccurate. The 1970 census, for example, gave the population of KwaMashu as 106 900 and that of Umlazi as 121 200. However, during the course of discussions with township officials it was acknowledged that the true figures were probably at least 50 per cent higher. Since KwaMashu is situated in the municipal area the pass laws apply and enable a tighter control to be exercised over illegal residents than in Umlazi which is in a homeland.[17] Officials estimated that the population of KwaMashu is approximately 170 000–200 000 and that of Umlazi approximately 200 000–250 000, while Lamont is said to contain 30 000 and Chesterville 15 000.[18] Houses which are planned for six persons usually contain 8–10 occupants. Thus there is a large undisclosed population of lodgers and what might be described as long-term visitors. Moreover, there are at least 25 000 unregistered domestic servants in Durban alone, living on private premises.[19] There appears all in all to be little prospect of a reasonably accurate enumeration of the urban African population as long as legal barriers to population mobility, which encourage census evasion, exist.

It is clear, therefore, that the provision of official low-cost housing for Africans in the DMA has not kept pace with the rate of rural–urban migration. This is evidenced not only by the above figures but also by the mushrooming shack settlements outside the Durban municipal area where African-occupied shacks have been eliminated. The new shack areas are located on the periphery of the built-up areas, often in valleys where they cannot easily be seen. They are centred mainly on the Pinetown magisterial district where unauthorized squatter settlements are found in the Mariannhill–Thornwood–Dassenhoek area and from Clermont stretching along the Umgeni River to the New Farm–Phoenix areas of the Inanda district north of KwaMashu.

No strict official control is exercised over migrants in these areas, and even in Clermont (Pinetown's African township with a 1970 census population of 25 800) tenancy is relatively uncontrolled. A study in Clermont in 1966 found a high frequency of overcrowding, often with one family per room; the occupancy rate then was 13,8 persons per dwelling compared with 6,6 in Umlazi, 7 in KwaMashu and Chesterville and 7,4 in Lamont.[20] The census figure for Clermont is grossly misleading, and the true population has been estimated at 60 000–75 000 of whom some 70 per cent are illegal residents.[21]

The growth of Clermont is indicative of the rapid influx of migrants to the Pinetown area. The estimated number of illegal squatters in this area rose from 5 000 in 1966 to 50 000 in 1969.[22] In addition to Clermont the Dassenhoek–Mariannhill area to the south of Pinetown contains an estimated 55 000–65 000 squatters,[23] while there are also unauthorized shack areas to the west of Pinetown for which no estimates are available.

A large shack community, estimated to number 100 000, is found along the Umgeni River between Inanda and Hillcrest. To the north of KwaMashu the shack population in the New Farm–Phoenix area was conservatively estimated at 60 000 in 1969.[24] There are no estimates for the squatter population to the south of Umlazi which has grown in recent years.

The total squatter population of the Durban–Pinetown area was estimated at 38 000 in 1965, 150 000 in 1969 and 250 000 in 1971.[25] Since then there has been a large and continuing influx of migrants and it is difficult to estimate the total African population of the DMA. Table 4.6 attempts to do this, but even then it excludes certain shack areas for which no estimates are available, while some of the high estimates are themselves conservative. The African population of the DMA could well approximate one million,[26] of whom at least 300 000 would be shack dwellers and almost 250 000 illegal residents in the four townships serving Durban. The re-emergence of shack areas and the overcrowding in the existing townships mean that any official low-cost housing programme in the DMA would probably have to cater for at least 600 000 Africans.

Table 4.6

ESTIMATED AFRICAN POPULATION, DURBAN METROPOLITAN AREA, 1973 ('000)[(a)]

	Low	High
KwaMashu	170	200
Lamont	30	30
Chesterville	15	15
Umlazi	200	250
Durban municipal hostels	11	11
State and private compounds—Durban	30	30
Private domestic servants—Durban	30	55
New Farm–Phoenix	60	60
Clermont	60	75
Dassenhoek–Mariannhill–Umhlatuzana	55	65
Umgeni valley (Inanda–Hillcrest)	100	100
	761	891

Note: (a) Excluding shack areas to the west of Pinetown and south of Umlazi.

Various estimates have been made of African housing requirements in the Durban area. On the basis of his 1966 study Watts estimated the shortfall of African houses in the DMA in 1972 at 8 000 but admitted that this was conservative particularly as the earlier survey had not established the number of illegally housed Africans.[27]

In 1965 the Durban Corporation carried out a detailed investigation into African housing needs for the ensuing fifteen years. This study was based on an assessment of the growth in African employment, taking into account the availability of White workers, sources of moneys for capital investment, industrial land resources and future demands in the different fields of employment. In 1968 figures were revised in the light of further information and the experience of the three intervening years. Whereas it was originally calculated that an additional 47 800 houses and 20 900 hostel beds would be required between 1965 and 1980,[28] the revised figures for 1968–80 were 11 500 houses and 63 660 hostel beds.[29] This represented a drastic reappraisal of the distribution of housing needs as between family and single accommodation. But the figures in respect of houses were based only on the number of male workers who qualified for family accommodation[30] and, since they excluded illegal residents, were an underestimate.

During fieldwork in early 1972 an official stated that 30 000 houses and 50 000 hostel beds were required immediately for Africans in the Durban area (excluding Pinetown). The cost of constructing a township house (including an allowance for the provision of services) is R2 000, so that family housing alone would demand an expenditure of R60 million.

These estimates, however, appear inadequate when compared with the United Nations target for areas experiencing rapid urbanization in developing countries.[31] This target of 15–18 dwellings per annum per 1 000 population is based on the rate of natural population growth, rural–urban migration, annual replacement and some allowance for compensating backlog. The application of this standard to the 1970 census African population of the DMA (395 000) results in an annual construction programme of 5 925–7 110 houses. But if underenumeration is borne in mind and a more realistic figure of even 800 000 Africans is used, we find that between 12 000 and 14 400 houses per annum would be required. For a population of one million annual housing requirements would be 15 000–18 000 dwellings, or in other words the construction each year of a new township the size of Kwa-Mashu.

The DMA is thought to present the most serious African housing problem in South Africa. The problem is compounded when the situation of the Indian and Coloured people as well as lower income Whites is considered. Watts estimated that, in 1966, 34 000 dwellings were required for non-Africans in the DMA.[32] Since then the housing shortage has almost certainly grown, and the re-emergence of large slum areas for all races cannot be discounted.

We have seen that such areas clearly exist in the case of Africans. Steps are being taken to alleviate the problem through the opening of new townships and hostels. Thus Ntuzuma, adjoining KwaMashu but situated in KwaZulu, has been developed and is planned to ultimately consist of 10 000 houses accommodating 50 000–60 000 persons, primarily illegal squatters from the shack areas in the vicinity. In the Pinetown area a new township called KwaNgendezi is to be developed at Dassenhoek to absorb the squatter population there. This is to contain 4 500 houses, and a further 3 500 are to be built at Salem and 8 000 at Clermont. Building is also continuing at Umlazi, and the scores of people who were reported to be sleeping in the bush adjoining the township early in 1972 have now apparently been accommodated. Additional hostels are to be constructed in the Pinetown area and Umlazi Glebe.

It is questionable, however, whether in the absence of a full-scale research project the true magnitude of the housing shortfall can be grasped. This has already been referred to by Watts, who made the further pertinent point that the government was devoting insufficient funds to housing.[33] Moreover, there is a serious shortage of essential urban services and public health and educational facilities in the DMA.

INFORMAL SECTOR HOUSING AS A SOLUTION?

The urban housing problem is universal. The position in Durban is paralleled in cities elsewhere in South Africa and throughout Africa. As Hance points out: 'the provision of housing . . . is the largest and most expensive urban need.'[34] He refers to the overcrowded and poorly constructed quarters of African cities and states that 'there are very few major cities where these conditions are not worsening despite some heroic efforts to move against the problem'.[35] He goes on to say: 'How to meet the housing needs of the present and burgeoning populations of most African cities is an almost insoluble dilemma. In no case to my knowledge is the housing program keeping up with the increasing population.'[36]

Such views of the urban housing problem are, however, predicated on the dismissal of informal or squatter settlements as a solution. Indeed, squatter areas are regarded by officialdom and the public alike as abounding with social problems. But studies in Peru indicate that such a view is 'grossly inaccurate';[37] there is in fact sufficient evidence in the rapidly urbanizing countries to show that squatter communities (known as *barriadas* in South America and *bidonvilles* in French-speaking Africa) are highly successful solutions to the problems of mass housing. The growing recognition of this fact is of special significance to our discussion in view of the large-scale re-emergence of shack settlements in the DMA.

Because of the rapid rate of urbanization in Africa, housing authorities are unable to provide new residential areas rapidly enough. But housing is no problem to migrants who build on unused land with whatever means and materials they can find. In Zambia, for example, it has been suggested that there is in reality no housing problem; rather, the shortage is in the amenities of urban living such as water supplies, sewerage, roads, transport, health and education.[38]

The loss of control over urban growth in many less-developed countries has been interpreted as a result of conflicts between government programmes and the demands of the people.[39] The ineffectiveness of urban planning and related low-income housing policies is due mainly to the ignorance of residential needs and priorities and to the consequent misunderstanding of the urban settlement process. Poverty alone cannot be blamed for poor environmental conditions; attempts to impose urban industrial middle-class standards upon the masses lead to large-scale squatting and to the bankruptcy of many official low-cost housing programmes.[40]

According to Turner[41] housing should be defined in terms of the dwelling environment and not in terms of dwelling structures, thus recognizing the relationship between man and environment. A good environment is not necessarily one of high physical standards.

Studies in various countries have shown that informal sector housing possesses many advantages. First, squatter areas usually have a more central location in relation to job opportunities and the cheapest food markets, Cato Manor being a good example. In contrast, residents in government projects lose time and money commuting and rents may be prohibitively high. Thus a centrally located shack provides a good environment however poor its material quality while mass housing provides a bad environment since it perpetuates poverty and thus blocks progress.[42]

Second, tenants in shack housing have greater mobility than in mass projects where they are tied to one permanent location. A rented shack or room can be given up at short notice and thus the occupier is free to move quickly to another more favourable location.[43]

Third, migrants prefer cheap housing in the informal sector to modern standard dwellings since the latter absorb a higher proportion of their income and make it more difficult for them to send their children to school.[44]

Fourth, squatter communities offer 'uniquely satisfactory opportunities'[45] for low-income migrants since they are characterized by the progressive development of dwellings. Families build their houses in stages as their resources permit, the more important elements first. They are free to act in accordance with their needs, and are able to provide more spacious buildings better adapted to their changing lifestyle; their investment in housing is synchronized with the rhythm of social and economic adaptation to the urban environment. In contrast, official policies and projects attempt to telescope the development process by requiring minimum modern standards, structures and installations; these policies aggravate the housing problem by disregarding the economic and social needs of the urban settlers.[46]

Fifth, whereas official housing programmes are characterized by long waiting-lists, squatters can occupy their plots immediately. This enables squatter families to improve their living conditions and become more independent at a much earlier and more active stage of life.[47]

But perhaps the most important advantage, which deserves to be considered separately, is the 'spontaneous mobilization of human and material resources'.[48] Squatters build their own houses from their own financial resources, and informal housing must be regarded as self-help community development by the poor.[49]

A major change in official policy is required so as to use public resources to harness the imagination, energy and financial resources of squatters.[50] At the same time the programme should harness the ideas of social workers, urban planners, architects and engineers. One solution is to channel the available resources into basic services along the lines of site-and-service schemes which are well known in Africa. Hance and Hellman describe their implementation in Lusaka and Soweto (the African township of Johannesburg) and they have been recommended for Kenya.[51] Under these schemes the local authority lays out the sites and provides the basic services such as water, sewerage and roads. Tenants are then permitted to erect temporary structures (perhaps with the aid of a loan from the local authority for the purchase of basic construction materials) at the back of the plot, leaving the front of the site vacant pending the provision of municipal housing. In the meantime tenants are required to maintain certain minimum standards. The site-and-service scheme was utilized during the early years of KwaMashu, but is perhaps best illustrated in the case of Soweto where the 35 000 shacks originally erected have all been replaced by houses.

A site-and-service housing programme can be divided into two parts,[52] viz. (i) contractor-installed services with the aid of central or local government funds and (ii) self-help services. So far as the infrastructure is concerned, experience in Zambia suggests that the lack of clean drinking-water, sewerage and roads were the major problems facing squatter communities, other facilities such as street lighting meriting a lower priority. In Zambia it appeared that the people were prepared to pay rates for services such as roads and water, and were in fact prepared to assist in their installation. An advantage of maximizing popular financial and physical effort in such programmes is that vandalism and disregard for publicly financed improvement measures are avoided.[53]

In the above discussion we have pointed to some of the disadvantages of official low-cost housing projects. There are, however, three more which must be mentioned. The first relates to costs. In Peru the financial cost of a *barriada* dwelling is less than one-half that of a low-cost housing unit. The difference is accounted for by the family performing various functions: contracting (thereby eliminating administrative overheads and profits), building without credit, designing and building without paying professional and legal fees, and avoiding building regulations.[54] In low-cost housing projects, on the other hand, the typical family is subjected to a maximum outlay during its period of minimum *per capita* income, and obtains less space *per capita*. Mass-housing projects thus conflict with the family's needs and means.

Second, the order of priorities for informal housing is the reverse of those for official housing.[55] The poor place more emphasis on security of tenure than on the physical condition of the dwelling whereas the government emphasizes the provision of a modern (but minimum) house. This represents an unconscious transference of middle-class values to the designs and plans for the poor and is the main reason for the failure of officials to realize the obvious potential of squatter housing.

Third, some of the concepts embedded in mass-housing schemes may be inapplicable in the context of rapid urbanization. In particular the imposition of foreign concepts of law and planning have been mentioned. For example, it is claimed that in Zambia laws relating to trading licences and renting rooms to lodgers are inapplicable in squatter areas, and that only by breaking the law has it been possible to evolve a relevant system for the conduct of day-to-day affairs. By existing independently of an imposed legal system the squatters have evolved a new lifestyle that is related to Africa; traditional values are extended into a new situation and a relevant urban culture has been evolved.[56]

In Africa the layout of mass housing differs from that of traditional village planning.[57] Planning concepts derived from the experience of developed countries are frequently inapplicable under circumstances typical in less-developed countries.[58]

Site-and-service schemes have several advantages over unauthorized squatter areas from an urban planning point of view. By providing an infrastructure, e.g. roads, they prevent unnecessary urban sprawl. They also enable greater control to be exercised in the co-ordinated planning of industrial location and urban growth.

Quite apart from alleviating the housing shortage, site-and-service schemes have favourable employment and linkage effects.[59] Squatter housing varies in standard from modest houses to makeshift shelters, and is the result of the creation of a local building industry. Although much of the building is undertaken by the family members themselves, the erection of single structures provides scope for small self-employed masons, carpenters, painters, etc., to establish themselves as entrepreneurs in the informal sector. Local builders provide less expensive

materials; the costs of building and maintenance are thus closer to the
means of the people and the buildings are capable of gradual improvement with more modern materials.[60] An alternative, and one which
has been the standard practice in site-and-service schemes, is for the
authorities to supply materials, e.g. concrete blocks, pipes, etc., at a
reasonable price. Local builders have a crucial role to play in the provision of informal sector housing and would benefit from specialized
assistance to improve their techniques and teach them basic costing
and design principles.

Apart from site-and-service schemes, another method of overcoming the urban housing problem is that of the emergency camp,
Cato Manor providing the leading example. This method, described
in chapter 1, closely resembles site-and-service schemes, but there is
an important difference, viz. it is not just the housing but the camp
itself which is temporary. An emergency camp is, in fact, to be established in the Pinetown area.

However, the impermanence of the emergency camp is a serious dis-
advantage. It represents a substantial expenditure, on the part of the
authorities as well as the squatters, in buildings and facilities which
are later demolished and dismantled. The residents are not motivated
to improve their dwellings—we noted in chapter 1 that Cato Manor
residents spent less on maintenance and improvements than those in
other areas—and thus the attainment of a standard of housing suitable
to the needs of the poor is delayed. Emergency camps do not provide
the residents with security of tenure, and they imply official disapproval
of permanent informal housing as a solution to the problem since they
are replaced by mass-housing schemes.

The implementation of either of these schemes would assist in eliminating the rent racketeering which is reported to be widespread in the
shack settlements in the DMA. For example, in 1965 it was reported
that in the Inanda squatter area adjoining KwaMashu the original
'owners' of shacks who had been rehoused in KwaMashu were subletting these shacks to new arrivals at rents of R6–12 per month. At
the time the rent in KwaMashu was only R6,50 per month so that
some owners were making substantial profits.[61] A similar position is
encountered in Clermont today where squatters are paying rentals of
R7–12 per month for shacks built of wood packaging and African
landlords are receiving R300–400 per month.[62] The emergence of
an exploitative landlord is a danger in squatter areas since by obtaining
such high returns on their investment they are encouraged to obtain
more land on which to erect shacks. They might thus be in a position
to corner the market by making it difficult for others to build themselves houses.

It should also be mentioned that demolition by the authorities of
shacks does not assist in solving the housing problem. The experience
of such measures in Cato Manor and in other parts of Africa shows

that the evicted squatter population merely moves to another part of the urban area. In Kenya the ILO mission found that demolition contributed to the low level of housing and sanitation in the informal sector; the threat of demolition discouraged squatters from constructing more substantial dwellings or from improving existing structures.[63] The mission was of the opinion that 'in view of the human suffering and considerable loss of capital involved, such policies are defensible only when combined with positive measures of improvement and promotion'.[64] As long as no alternative housing is available, demolition merely destroys the existing housing and dislocates families. Thus the police raids and demolition of shacks at New Farm, Dassenhoek and other squatter areas in the DMA can only exacerbate an already serious housing shortage.

Much of the above discussion is, however, more applicable to a less-developed country than to an intermediate country such as South Africa. In chapter 6 we shall examine some aspects of income distribution in South Africa, but in the meantime we need to consider what the housing aspirations of urban Africans are and whether we can really recommend site-and-service housing in the DMA.

The establishment of mass-housing schemes poses funding problems in all countries. The financing of such schemes for Africans in South Africa could be facilitated by a change in policy involving the radical reallocation of resources, but even then a substantial budgetary allocation for housing would be required.

In this connection it is interesting to compare South Africa and Zambia. It has been stated that it is economically impossible to give every Zambian a European-type house.[65] However, a 'European' house in a 'European' street is still regarded by most people as the desired solution despite the fact that squatters in Lusaka have 'evolved a planning philosophy that is based firmly on traditional values, modified to suit urban conditions. They have evolved the first post-colonial planning system.'[66]

But in South Africa, with its longer tradition and greater degree of African urbanization and its more modern urban industrial economy, does this argument apply to the same extent? Do urban Africans aspire to the European-style houses of White Durban or would they be content with the site-and-service approach? And would the income redistribution and welfare aspects be satisfied by site-and-service housing?

In Durban studies among the Indian community (which is considerably more urbanized and possesses a higher *per capita* income and a higher status in the racial hierarchy than the African) suggest that the low-income groups are prepared to accept substandard housing because of the low accommodation costs which enable them to save and later move to other housing. Indians whose residential pattern has been dislocated by the Group Areas Act are happier in Tintown, a site-and-service camp, than in Chatsworth, a mass-housing scheme, because of the lower rentals and more central location. Moreover, they are a more homogeneous community. In fact, there is a discernible move among low-income family units out of Chatsworth to shack areas in Inanda on the urban periphery. There is no reason to believe that the African migrant would adopt a different view, so that site-and-service schemes should satisfy his aspirations, in the short-term at any rate.

The income redistribution aspects can then be satisfied by the provision of urban services in these areas. In addition to water, sewerage and streets, the schemes would require health, education, transport, recreation, street lighting and community facilities on a more generous basis than were provided in Cato Manor. In addition, the authorities could supply building materials at cost price as was done, for example, in the Cato Manor Emergency Camp.

Concurrently with a site-and-service programme, mass housing could be provided for Africans (probably those who are more integrated into the urban community) who can afford the rentals and who would prefer the more modern facilities and layout of these schemes. The prevention of unnecessary urban sprawl is, however, an important issue in a metropolitan area; the Indian community is in the process of making the transition to living in high-rise apartment blocks and there is no doubt that the provision of such buildings in African residential areas will ultimately have to be considered.

A further issue is whether we can allow dual planning and legal standards in the DMA. It is important to note that certain minimum standards are laid down in site-and-service schemes, so that there need be no conflict with municipal planning regulations. When we consider the question of dual legal standards, a more generous granting of licences to hawkers, pedlars and small traders and artisans, and a more relaxed attitude to lodgers, would do much to facilitate relationships between the authorities and the community and to improve the latter's respect for the law. The authorities should recognize that the informal sector fulfils a real need for its members.

ETHNIC SEGREGATION

This discussion of resettlement would be incomplete without mentioning that the official segregation policy is pursued to its limits in urban townships by separating the various African ethnic groups.

As soon as houses became available at Umlazi in 1962 the policy was adopted of settling there only Zulu employed at the Point and south of Berea Road; all other Zulu were resettled at KwaMashu, with the exception of a relatively small number of families with very low incomes who were settled in subeconomic houses at Chesterville and Lamont. Those Zulu who were moved before houses at Umlazi became available, and employed at the Point or south of Berea Road, could elect to be moved later to Umlazi. Figures available for the period 1 September 1965 to 31 December 1969 show that 149 families transferred from KwaMashu to Umlazi, but during the same period only three families transferred from Umlazi to KwaMashu.

From March 1968 these two townships were closed to non-Zulu, who are now diverted to Lamont and Chesterville as vacancies arise. Thus the existing position is that Zulu are to reside in Umlazi and KwaMashu and other ethnic groups in Lamont and Chesterville. This process will take some time; in August 1970, 83,4 per cent of those in family accommodation in Lamont and Chesterville were Zulu compared with 90,3 per cent in KwaMashu. Zulu comprised 94,4 per cent of single men in hostels in KwaMashu compared with 83,3 per cent in hostels and compounds elsewhere in Durban.

Overall, Zulu comprised 90 per cent of the African population accommodated in the Durban municipal area, accounting for approximately 89 per cent of those in family housing in the townships, and slightly over 90 per cent of those in single, state and private accommodation. Xhosa from the Transkei are the second main group (6,1 per cent); they are chiefly migrants as can be seen from the fact that they are relatively more important in non-family housing, comprising over 8 per cent of those in single, state and private accommodation compared with less than 5 per cent in family housing.

NOTES AND REFERENCES

1 Figures in this and succeeding sections were obtained from the City of Durban *Mayor's Minute* (annual) for the years 1958–67, and the *Annual Report of the Medical Officer of Health*, 1961–4.

2 According to the *Natal Daily News* of 15 June 1960, the Cato Manor Welfare and Development Board reported that in 1959 in Cato Manor and Chesterville there were 686 cases of housebreaking, 400 of robbery and 967 of theft (in addition to 2 109 common assaults, 1 332 serious assaults, 76 murders and 80 rape cases).

3 This boycott resulted in municipal 'KB' sales declining from 5,1 million gallons in 1958–9 to 4,5 million gallons in 1959–60. For a description of the tense political climate prevailing in 1959, see Leo Kuper, *An African Bourgeoisie*, New Haven: Yale University Press, 1965, pp. 9–20.

4 For the record these areas were Ezinkaweni, Mnyasana, Emhlangeni, Newtown, Ntabashishi, Madhlebe, Bellair Road, Wiggins Road, Mgangeni, Mpompeni, Tibela, North Bank Road, Ridgeview, Mkalandodo, and Banki.

5 For a description of Chateau and Good Hope Estates see *The Durban Housing Survey*, op. cit., pp. 300–2.

6 Cabazini, Dhlamini, Ezimbuzeni, Fairbreeze, Jeepcoat, Mgenge, Manasa, Mokoena, Mathonsi, Ndhlovu, Nsimbini and Orlando.

7 Happy Valley is still a shack area, the Africans having been replaced by Coloureds (*Natal Mercury*, 26 March 1973).

8 City of Durban *Mayor's Minute*, 1961, p. 22.

9 The figures in the tables relating to accommodation are taken from the annual returns of the municipal Department of Bantu Administration, those concerning Umlazi being provided by the City Engineer; 1970 was the last year for which figures were available.

10 Occupiers of houses are permitted to take in lodgers who must be registered, the lodging charge being prescribed. It is known that there are many unregistered lodgers who probably pay more than the prescribed charge.

11 Single in this context means the number of beds in hostels but does not necessarily mean unmarried.

12 This was popularly known as the 'locations in the sky' Act.

13 Hance, op. cit., p. 292.

14 Margaret A. Young, *A Study of the Social Circumstances and Characteristics of Bantu in the Durban Region*, Report No. 1, Durban: Institute for Social Research, University of Natal, 1965, p. 73.

15 Sadie, op. cit., p. 206.

16 City of Durban *Mayor's Minute* (annual).

17 It should be noted that South Africa's influx control and 'endorsing out' system of controlling rural–urban migration has its parallel elsewhere in Africa, e.g. Niger, Congo (Brazzaville), Zaïre, Kenya, Tanzania and Ghana. See Hance, op. cit., pp. 277–8. The use of the official term 'homeland' in Part II does not imply that the authors identify with the concept.

18 See also the *Natal Mercury*, 5 April 1973.

19 Ibid.

20 H. L. Watts, R. J. Davies & G. H. Waters, *The Spatial Distribution of the Present and Future Residential Population of Metropolitan Durban*, Institute for Social Research, University of Natal, 1967, p. 25. The figure of 8–10 persons per dwelling quoted two paragraphs earlier suggests a deterioration in these townships since 1966.

21 *Natal Mercury*, 20 April 1972 and 5 April 1973, *Daily News*, 19 January 1973.

22 *Natal Mercury*, 9 April 1969.

23 *Natal Mercury*, 5 April 1973.

24 *Natal Mercury*, 3 April 1969.

25 *Natal Mercury*, 3 April 1969 and 21 January 1971.

26 See the estimates in the *Natal Mercury*, 5 April 1973.

27 H. L. Watts, 'Housing and Human Needs in South Africa', paper presented at the Annual Council Meeting of the South African Institute of Race Relations, Durban, 11–14 January 1972, p. 2.

28 Durban Corporation City Engineer's Department, *Bantu Housing Investigation*, 1966, pp. 44–5.

29 A report of the Durban Corporation Bantu Administration Department, 20 November 1968.

30 The qualification for family housing is ten years continuous employment in Durban or 15 years' residence in Durban if employment is broken.

31 ILO, op. cit., p. 475.

32 Watts, op. cit., p. 2.

33 Ibid, p. 3.

34 Hance, op. cit., p. 283.

35 Ibid.

36 Ibid, p. 286.

37 William Mangin & John C. Turner, 'The Barriada Movement', *Progressive Architecture*, May 1968, p. 155.

38 'Upgrading Kapwepwe Suburb: A Project Proposal', Kafue: American Friends Service Committee, n.d., p.1.

39 John C. Turner, 'Housing Priorities, Settlement Patterns, and Urban Development in Modernizing Countries', *Journal of the American Institute of Planners*, vol. 34 no. 6, November 1968, p. 354.

40 Ibid., p. 355.

41 Ibid.

42 Mangin & Turner, op. cit., p. 158.

43 Turner, op. cit., p. 355.

44 Ibid., p. 356.

45 John C. Turner, 'Barriers and Channels for Housing Development in Modernizing Countries', *Journal of the American Institute of Planners*, vol. 33 no. 3, May 1967, p. 167.

46 Ibid.

47 Ibid., p. 176.

48 Ibid.

49 Mangin & Turner, op. cit., p. 161.

50 'Upgrading . . .', op. cit., p. 11.

51 Ibid., p. 290, Ellen Hellman, *Soweto: Johannesburg's African City*, Johannesburg: South African Institute of Race Relations, 1971, and ILO, op, cit., p. 199.

52 Andrew *et al.*, op. cit., p. 22.

53 Ibid., p. 21.

54 Mangin & Turner, op. cit., p. 159.

55 Turner, 'Barriers and . . .', op. cit., p. 179.

56 Andrew *et al.*, op. cit., p. 25.

57 Ibid., p. 19.

58 Turner, 'Barriers and . . .', op. cit., p. 167.

59 ILO, op. cit., p. 199.

60 Thomas L. Blair, 'Shelter in Urbanising and Industrialising Africa', in Paul Oliver (ed.), *Shelter in Africa*, London: Barrie & Jenkins, 1971, p. 231.

61 *Natal Mercury*, 5 February 1965.

62 *Sunday Tribune*, 23 April 1972, and *Daily News*, 19 January 1973.

63 ILO, op. cit., p. 227.

64 Ibid.

65 'Upgrading . . .', op. cit., p. 2.

66 Paul Andrew, Malcolm Christie & Richard Martin, 'Squatter Manifesto', *Ekistics*, 201, August 1972, p. 113.

CHAPTER 5

The Townships Today

Having described the resettlement of the African community in the new townships and the general housing position, we now proceed to examine the financing and provision of services and facilities in these townships.[1]

ADMINISTRATION AND FINANCE

The administration of the five African townships primarily serving Durban is complex. Umlazi and the newly-established Ntuzuma are both situated in the 'homelands' and are consequently controlled by the central government. Prior to August 1973 KwaMashu, Lamont and Chesterville were situated within the municipal area and were administered by the Durban Corporation. But, as mentioned in chapter 4, the position has now changed with regard to these latter townships, which have been removed from the control of the Corporation and are now administered by a Bantu Affairs Administration Board.

The Bantu Affairs Administration Act No. 45 of 1971 provided for the establishment of such boards to replace the Bantu Administration departments of local authorities throughout South Africa. The official aim of this legislation is to improve administrative efficiency and the mobility of labour. It is claimed that bureaucratic red tape will be reduced and that since there will be only 26 boards liaison with the government will be improved. However, the administration of African townships was perhaps the only major area in which the central government did not exercise direct control over the lives of the African population. In terms of apartheid ideology it can be argued that the seizure of township control was a logical and inevitable step; in important centres such as Durban, Pietermaritzburg, Johannesburg, Cape Town, Port Elizabeth and East London the city councils are controlled by non-Nationalists so that, despite the fact that local authorities are obliged to implement government legislation, the application of policy from the National Party's point of view would be facilitated by direct control. The boards have the status of local authorities; their members are nominated by specific organizations (such as local authorities and organized commerce and industry) and are appointed by the government.[2]

Whilst the authoritarian aspects of the legislation have been criticized, the greater mobility of labour allowed has been recognized as an improvement on the previous position.[3] Africans living in one area may now obtain employment in another area under a board's jurisdiction without losing their residential qualifications and since these boards cover large areas—the Port Natal Board, for instance, covers Durban and seven other magisterial districts—it appears that labour mobility could be increased.

The boards are responsible for African affairs in White areas only. Thus Umlazi does not fall under the Port Natal Board, and the board's control of KwaMashu will cease when this township is incorporated into KwaZulu in 1975. The boards take over the assets, liabilities, responsibilities, revenue and staff of the municipal Bantu Administration departments. In Durban the Corporation is continuing to administer the townships until such time as the Port Natal Board's head office is functional. Thus in practice the position is so far unchanged, and since the board is to take over the Corporation's Bantu Revenue Account, the following discussion still applies despite the fact that the data collected relate to the position prior to the take-over.

The provision of housing, services and facilities in African townships may be financed from three main sources, viz. (i) the Bantu Revenue Account of the local authority (under which term we now include Bantu Affairs Administration boards), (ii) general rates, and (iii) a tax on employers who do not provide housing. We shall examine each of these sources in turn.

THE BANTU REVENUE ACCOUNT

The major source of revenue for township administration is the Bantu Revenue Account.[4] In 1970 the Corporation's Bantu Revenue Account budget amounted to over R1 million on capital account and approximately R10 million on revenue account.[5] The latter figure represents 11 per cent of total borough expenditure. An important feature is that township administration was financially self-sufficient, making no demands on the revenue of borough funds. Moreover, the account was virtually a state trust account since all expenditure, capital and revenue required the prior approval of the Minister of Bantu Administration and Development. Such approval could, however, be anticipated for recurrent items of revenue expenditure as well as for previously approved capital schemes. A summary of the income and expenditure on this account is shown in Table 5.1.

This table shows that the Bantu Revenue Account pivots largely on the profits on the sale of beer. The local authority has a mono-poly on the manufacture and sale of 'KB', and we have already noted (p. 11) that as far back as 1908 legislation permitted the profits to be utilized for the provision of housing and other facilities for Africans. The relevant controlling Act today is the Bantu Beer Act No. 63 of 1962. The uses of profits are specified—one-third for welfare and social amenities and, as far as housing schemes and hostels are concerned, two-thirds for capital expenditure (including services), interest and redemption charges and maintenance costs.

The brewing of 'KB' has developed into a major public enterprise

Table 5.1

SUMMARY OF THE BANTU REVENUE ACCOUNT FOR THE YEAR ENDED 31 JULY 1970

Item	Amount (R'000)		
	Income	Expenditure	Surplus (+)/ Deficit (−)
Breweries and beerhalls	5 811	4 538	+1 273
Liquor	962	948	+ 14
Recreation and Welfare	17	417	− 400
Housing	2 084	3 025	− 941
General	768	598	+ 170
Total	9 642	9 526	+ 116

Source: City Treasurer's Report and Abstract of Accounts, 1970

in Durban—an activity which in any other market economy would be confined to the private sector. In 1948–9 the Corporation beerhalls sold 2,36 million gallons. This increased to 4,42 million gallons in 1954–5 and 11,4 million gallons in 1964–5. Despite the availability of 'European' liquor since 1962, the consumption of 'KB' has increased rapidly, sales totalling 26,94 million gallons in 1969–70 and 28,76 million gallons in 1971–2. It can be seen from Table 5.1 that profits on the manufacture and sale of beer almost covered the losses on housing and recreation and welfare. In the previous financial year the profits exceeded the sum of the losses on these services by R124 000.

We have also noted (chapter 3) that the Liquor Amendment Act No. 72 of 1961, which came into operation in 1962, enabled Africans to purchase 'European' liquor. The local authorities were given the monopoly on the sale of liquor in the townships; 20 per cent of the profits are devoted to social and recreational services in the same way as surpluses from the beer account, and the remainder is paid to the government for homeland development.

Most of the revenue of R17 000 in the recreation and welfare category is accounted for by a contra entry of R15 000 for ambulance fees. The only revenue of any significance is receipts from the hire of recreation grounds, viz. R1 889. Expenditure in this category is allocated mainly to administration, social services, recreation and sports grounds. Grants constitute a significant portion of administration costs, and are made annually to a wide variety of institutions directly or indirectly concerned in promoting welfare. Other items of expenditure, which indicate the wide range of functions and benefits, are milk distribution relief, children's parties and parcels, relief for indigents, dried milk for mothers, garden and house competitions and the KwaMashu Show.

The second major source of income on the Bantu Revenue Account relates to rentals derived from family houses and hostels. Income from rentals is, however, insufficient to cover expenditure on housing. Sub-economic housing schemes are based on low rates of interest, the shortfall being made good by the state and the charging of low rentals which are determined according to the income of the occupiers. Economic schemes, which include hostels, are based on market rates of interest (in practice usually fractionally smaller), rentals being calcu-lated to cover the cost of interest and redemption. In both cases, however, additional costs are incurred in administration and other items.

To cover these losses there has been a succession of varied arrange-ments and formulae determined by the state for sharing the losses between the state and the local authority. These have necessitated an arduous and complex system of accounts, further complicated by the periodic government policy declarations issued to local authorities. Recently, this has been somewhat ameliorated by the conversion of all subeconomic schemes to economic schemes as from 31 March 1970. This has clarified, on a more permanent basis, the local authorities' share of losses, but not reduced it, and has not affected subeconomic rentals.[6] The sources of revenue used to defray losses on housing have already been indicated. In 1970 expenditure on economic housing amounted to almost R2,5 million and on subeconomic housing R536 000, while income totalled R1,8 million and R271 000 respec-tively. Thus there were losses of almost R0,7 million on economic housing (or 27 per cent of expenditure in that category) and R265 000 on subeconomic housing (or almost 50 per cent of expenditure).

The General Account relates mainly to the registration of African employees and the administration and enforcement of influx control, the costs of registration and of the inspectorate comprising practically all the expenditure.[7] Registration fees constitute 53 per cent of the income and fines 18 per cent.

SUBSIDIZATION FROM GENERAL RATES

We have already alluded to the fact that the Bantu Revenue Account was self-sufficient and was not subsidized out of the Borough Fund, the main sources of income of which are property taxes (rates) and user charges. The independence of the Bantu Revenue Account illustrates a principle long enshrined in South African local government finance, viz. that the provision of African housing and services should make no demands on general municipal revenue.

This principle was not enshrined by statute but was adhered to by many local authorities, of which Durban was one. Prior to the creation of the Bantu Affairs Administration Board, only 21 of the more than 450 local authorities in South Africa were subsidizing their Bantu revenue accounts.[8] In Durban the Bantu Revenue Account was not always in a healthy position; in 1952, for example, the fear was expressed that unless assistance was received in the field of housing 'Durban will in the not too distant future join the cities whose ratepayers contribute, in some cases substantially, to the Native Revenue Account'.[9]

The burden of African housing and township services in Durban has been borne not by the ratepayers (who are mainly White but include a fair proportion of Indians and in whose houses, offices and factories the Africans supply vital labour). Rather it is borne by the Africans themselves, in effect from municipal beer profits. In other words, the more liquor (particularly beer) an African purchases from the municipality the better is his chance of having a proper roof over his head, a clinic, a crèche, a sportsfield and a cinema.

The position in Durban may be contrasted with that obtaining in Johannesburg where expenditure on Bantu Revenue Account has consistently exceeded income. Since 1941 the Johannesburg municipality has met this deficit from general rates;[10] in 1971–2 the subsidy amounted to R2,5 million.[11]

Local governments have a triple budget function, viz. allocation, distribution and stabilization.[12] It has been strongly argued that their main concern should be with the allocation of resources rather than with bringing about desired changes in income distribution.[13] It is clear that the local authorities in Durban failed in both respects. Not only did they fail to effect a redistribution of income towards the Africans (and Blacks generally), but they failed to allocate sufficient public goods and services to these communities, as will be shown later in this chapter. As indicated earlier in this chapter, this position will not be altered under the Bantu Administration boards and the new system thus perpetuates the inequalities of the past.

TAX ON EMPLOYERS

The Bantu Services Levy Act No. 25 of 1952 enforced a direct contribution to the costs of housing from employers of African males, other than domestic servants, who did not provide housing. The rate levied is 20 cents per week per employee. Revenue from the levy may be allocated to expenditure on the provision of water, sanitation, lighting and road services to the boundary of a location or hostel, or to the cost of interest and redemption charges in respect of any loan raised to finance such works or services, and to expenditure on rudimentary services within a location. Funds may also be allocated for the same purposes from this account to any other body or local authority housing males employed in the urban area. During the 1969–70 Durban Corporation financial year income totalled R1 758 000 and expenditure R1 761 000. Levy collections from employers in Durban exceeded R1 million, the balance of the income consisting of advances from the South African Bantu Trust in respect of the provision of services at Umlazi and Ntuzuma which were undertaken by the Corporation as agent for the government.

This Act was replaced by the Contributions in Respect of Bantu Labour Act No. 29 of 1972. In terms of the new legislation the funds collected can be used for the maintenance of the services and not merely for their provision.

STATE ASSISTANCE

In addition to these three main sources of finance discussed above, certain assistance is obtained from the central government in respect of housing. Although the Housing Act No. 35 of 1920 made local authorities responsible for the provision of dwellings for low-income groups, it has always been clear that large subeconomic housing schemes could be introduced only if the State shared the financial burden.

However, it was not until 1934 that the central government made available loans to the local authorities for subeconomic schemes for Africans. The proposed State Native Housing Scheme to assist local authorities did not survive the change of government in 1948, and the present position is that the National Housing Fund makes available loans to local authorities via the Bantu Housing Board. Subeconomic housing for Africans has been abolished and in 1972 the government reaffirmed that it was not prepared to reintroduce such housing on the grounds that existing rentals are reasonable and transport and other services are subsidized.[14] Rather, government priorities are for bachelor hostels in the townships and family housing in the 'homelands'. In this respect Durban is perhaps more fortunate than cities such as Johannesburg in that Umlazi is situated in the KwaZulu homeland and is therefore on the priority list for housing. Local authorities are finding it increasingly difficult to obtain loans from the central government for family housing. In 1972–3 R5,95 million was provided by the National Housing Fund for African housing in urban areas, Durban's allocation amounting to only R69 600.[15]

In the foregoing consideration of the Bantu Revenue Account reference to reserves, interest and transfer entries has, for the purposes of clarity, been omitted. They are, however, an important part of the accounts and some reference to them is necessary. The 1970 Balance Sheet showed a capital surplus of over R12 million, which represents that portion of the existing assets of the Bantu Revenue Account that has been repaid. There are five reserve accounts, the total accumulated surplus amounting to almost R5,1 million in July 1970 while interest for the financial year totalled R279 000. This surplus is represented by external investment at market rates of interest and internal loans at a fractionally lower rate.

It may appear that these reserves are large, particularly in relation to the total budget. However, there is little doubt that large reserves are necessary if the Bantu Revenue Account is to continue to be self-sufficient. Further, the investments provide substantial revenue and act as a buffer against new developments and changes in policy. In addition to these reserves, trust account reserves (and investments) total R700 000.[16]

Thus far we have discussed only the townships hitherto administered by the Durban Corporation. The position is somewhat different in the case of Umlazi since it falls within a 'homeland' where townships are financed largely by the South African Bantu Trust. The Trust in turn derives its funds largely from parliamentary appropriations. But the local authorities (through their Bantu revenue accounts) also contribute to 'homeland' township development; we have already alluded to the fact that local authorities are obliged to channel 80 per cent of their profits on the sale of hard liquor to the Department of Bantu Administration and Development for use in the 'homelands', while services are financed from the Bantu Services Levy Fund.

RENTALS AND SERVICES

There has been no change in accommodation costs since 1959 in the townships hitherto administered by the Durban Corporation. Thus, after the initial burden of increased accommodation costs was absorbed by the resettled population of the shack areas, these costs became stabilized. This has constituted an important contribution to the increase in the real income of African households. We shall now discuss the rental position in each township in turn.

In February 1971 *KwaMashu* contained 15 385 houses and a hostel with 17 000 beds. The houses were mainly part of a letting scheme, monthly rentals amounting to R3,32 for a two-roomed semi-detached house and R6,28 for a four-roomed house. However, there is also a home-ownership scheme (local authority loans are advanced for houses up to R900 in value but beyond that the owner pays in full) as well as a selling scheme for which monthly instalments were slightly lower than rentals. In 1971 there were only 49 owner-built dwellings but 5 351 houses had been purchased under the selling scheme.

Chesterville is situated about eight kilometres inland from the city centre on 282 acres (113 ha), and comprises 1 265 four-roomed houses with monthly rentals ranging from a subeconomic minimum of R2,75 to an economic rent of R9,95. The houses consist of three rooms and a kitchen.

Lamont, the oldest township, covers an area of 1 093 acres (437 ha). Its 2 762 houses consist of 1 911 two- to four-roomed dwellings which are let either at subeconomic (R1,25–6,00 per month) or economic (R8,85–10,85 per month) rentals, and 851 houses in an economic home-ownership scheme. The latter comprises 107 owner-built houses under a loan scheme, and 62 detached and 682 semi-detached houses built under a selling scheme.

Closely associated with Lamont, and adjoining it, is the S. J. Smith Hostel. This consists of 16 residential blocks on 44 acres (18 ha). In 1967 it housed 4 652 males (this has subsequently been reduced to

4 481) of whom 432 occupied single rooms at R5,20 per month,
1 462 were in rooms of three to four beds at R3,10 per month, 2 445
were in rooms of nine to ten beds at R2,35 per month and 313 were
accommodated in large dormitories at R2,35 per month.[17]

Umlazi Glebe, which consists of 195 acres (78 ha), originally provided
family housing but since 1968 has been converted to a hostel scheme
for men. Rentals range from R3,50 to R4,00 per month.

Umlazi is situated in the 'homeland' and land can therefore be held
on a freehold basis. It covers an area of 7 500 acres (3 000 ha) and is
planned to contain 22 000 houses when fully developed. By May 1971,
18 693 houses had been built of which 62 were owner-built. The infor-
·mation available shows that 3 059 sites, including those for owner-
building, had been sold by the end of 1971. This means that approximately 3 000 houses had been purchased. Purchase prices range from
R16,00 to R42,00 per site and the houses are valued at R575. The
monthly cost to the occupier is R5,75, which covers all costs including
land, with a redemption period of 40 years. Provision has also been
made for owner-built sites for the more affluent, who can then build
to their own design. But the great majority of Umlazi residents rent
their dwellings, and monthly rentals, originally R6,10 to R6,72 (according to the size of plot) were advanced in 1968 to R6,72 and R7,02.
This includes water, which is free.

It should be mentioned that at Lamont and Chesterville rent is in
practice charged on a sliding scale based on the tenant's earnings in the
preceding year. In Lamont in the past four years there have been no
evictions for non-payment of rent; instead the authorities have resorted
to the use of stop-orders.

Apart from accommodation, other services normally provided by
local authorities are electricity, water and sewerage. Chesterville has
metered electricity throughout, as do all hostels. Although electricity
is available to all townships it is not generally supplied; for example,
there was a trade–off between the provision of housing and electricity
at Umlazi. As a consequence those people who were moved from
Umlazi Glebe in 1968 were unable to use their electrical appliances.
In KwaMashu the authorities found that the majority of households
could not afford the average monthly electricity bill of R1,50;
the supply of electricity therefore became uneconomical and was
stopped after an initial experimental scheme which covered 1 250
houses.

There is an individual piped water supply in all townships. In the
former Corporation townships water is metered at the rate of 17 cents
per 1 000 gallons. Originally water in Lamont and Chesterville was
not metered and the average household consumption of 7 000–9 000
gallons per month was considered excessive in relation to the average for
Whites in Durban of 6 000–8 000 gallons. Once meters were installed
consumption declined to an average of 4 000–4 500 in these two town-

ships. In KwaMashu it is reported to be only 3 000 gallons. All township houses are provided with showers and waterborne sanitation.

TRANSPORT

Transport between the townships and central points in Durban is provided mainly by railway and bus services. There are no municipal records of African car ownership, but relatively few members of this community possess cars: in Umlazi, for example, there are only 2 600 registered vehicles.

RAIL

The provision of railway services to KwaMashu and Umlazi entailed the construction of spurs to existing lines at a cost of approximately R1,25 and R5 million respectively. The former service was inaugurated in December 1962 and provides 61 trains in each direction per day. The latter, starting with a limited service of 18 trains per day in January 1968, had a full service of 58 trains per day in operation by April 1968; during the peak hours trains run at three-minute intervals. Rail fares are subsidized and the South African Railways estimated that in 1972–3 a loss of R16,3 million would be incurred in operating passenger services to Black townships in South Africa.

The ability of the rail services to meet the demand for transport can be measured by an estimate of the number of township residents in employment. This is assessed by taking into account the number of households, the average number of earners per household, and the hostel accommodation for single persons. On this basis there were, on 31 July 1970, 42 212 economically active persons residing in Kwa-Mashu and 37 250 in Umlazi. The South African Railways takes a count, on one specific day of each year, of the number of passengers utilizing the township rail services, travelling in one direction only. On 22 October 1970, the count was 44 102 for KwaMashu and 46 230 for Umlazi. Travelling to and from work constitutes, of course, only part of the demand for transport. However, rail services clearly have the capacity to supply the needs of the disclosed working population of the two townships; the position is less clear when illegal residents are taken into account. Moreover, an unquantifiable number of unregistered workers may have been excluded in the above calculation of the economically active population.

BUS

The Bantu Transport Services Act No. 53 of 1957 (amended by Act No. 11 of 1972) provides for a weekly levy of 10 cents on the same basis and with the same exceptions as the Services Levy. The 1972 amendment provided that employers would have to make contributions for female as well as male employees.

All receipts on this account are paid to the Secretary for Transport, who reimburses the local authority with an amount to cover adminis-

trative costs on the basis of a formula. The Secretary for Transport
pays these accruals into the Consolidated Revenue Fund and may use
such moneys to subsidize transport companies carrying African passengers within the local authority's area of jurisdiction. In the 1969–70
financial year the income from this levy in Durban totalled R525 000
of which R515 000 accrued to the Secretary for Transport.

Rail services are complemented by a comprehensive network of
bus services. The rail and bus network in Umlazi is depicted in Map 4,
which shows that most parts of the township are within easy walking
distance of either a bus route or a railway station. A similar position
obtains in KwaMashu.

Putco (Public Utility Transport Corporation) operates inside the
townships, and from them to various points in Durban, for example,
between KwaMashu and the Point and between Umlazi and Fynnlands.
A special market service is operated for women. *Putco* also operates
in the Pinetown area and in the Eston–Umbumbulu–Umbogintwini–
Isipingo area. Figures are not available to enable a comparison to be
made with rail services. However, in the year ended 28 February 1972,
Putco carried 25 411 676 passengers. If Sundays are excluded, this
gives a figure of 41 000 passengers per day travelling in one direction.
The KwaMashu–Point service alone carries 11 000 passengers per day
in each direction.

The Durban Municipality operates a wide network of bus services,
which includes internal routes, in Durban and the Pinetown area. The
main routes for Africans living in the townships are those between
Umlazi, Lamont, Chesterville and Pinetown and the Durban central,
Jacobs and Bluff industrial points. Figures indicating the magnitude of
these services are not available, but they clearly comprise an important
component of the transport system as a whole.

In addition to the above, fleets of privately-owned Indian and African
buses operate between the townships and the city. However, it is the
policy of the municipality to take over companies which run buses
on routes on which the municipality operates. Finally, there are the
private taxis operated by Africans within the townships and points
in the city.

COSTS

In the PDL calculation in the following chapter the monthly rail
season fare of R2,85 from the KwaMashu and Umlazi termini to
Durban central is used as representing the cheapest form of travel,
equivalent to about 6 cents per journey. The bus fare for the same
journey is 10 cents. Bus passengers prefer to make the larger payment
for convenience and timesaving at the points of embarkation and/or
disembarkation.

Obviously transport costs differ in relation to the location of residence
and employment.[18] Those who work in the townships may have no

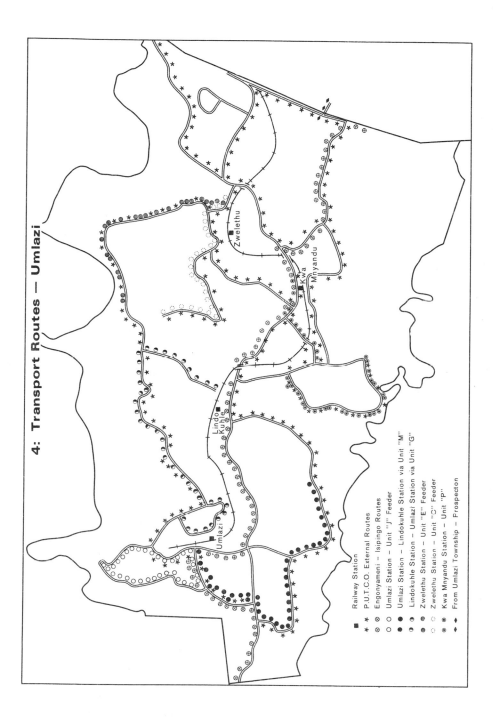

4: Transport Routes — Umlazi

- ■ Railway Station
- ✴ ✴ P.U.T.C.O. External Routes
- ⊗ ⊗ Engonyameni – Isipingo Routes
- ○ ○ Umlazi Station – Unit "J" Feeder
- ● ● Umlazi Station – Lindokuhle Station via Unit "M"
- ◉ ◉ Lindokuhle Station – Umlazi Station via Unit "G"
- ◉ ◉ Zwelethu Station – Unit "E" Feeder
- ◌ ◌ Zwelethu Station – Unit "C" Feeder
- ◉ ◉ Kwa Mnyandu Station – Unit "P"
- ✦ ✦ From Umlazi Township – Prospecton

transport costs, while the fare from the smaller townships to the city is 5 or 6 cents. On the other hand, workers may be involved in three journeys in each direction daily. An example of the latter is a messenger employed by the University of Natal whose monthly transport cost is R8,87. Being a single man he can perhaps afford this cost. The alternative, which would probably apply if he were married, would be to walk between the termini and home and place of employment. Such cases involve rising early and getting home late.

AMENITIES AND FACILITIES

The purpose of this section is to examine the amenities and facilities —health, welfare, recreational and other—provided in the townships.

HEALTH

The main hospital for Africans in Durban is King Edward VIII, which also serves the Indian community.[19] Statistics at this hospital indicate a marked improvement in general health conditions over the years.

Between 1961 and 1969 the number of tuberculosis notifications at this hospital declined from 1 648 to 1 234, the attack rate per 1 000 people from 3,78 to 2,66, and deaths from 129 to 50.[20] According to the City Medical Officer of Health, ' . . . the continually improving standard of living of urban Africans makes them less prone to the disease which is also being diagnosed at an earlier stage than some years ago. But the same cannot be said of rural Africans who come to Durban to attend clinics; they are often extremely ill and require immediate hospitalisation.'[21]

Dysentery and gastro-enteritis have been a common cause of death among urban Africans. The number of deaths from these causes at King Edward VIII Hospital fell from 532 in 1960 to 137 in 1969, the annual average being 336 during the first half of the decade and 211 in the second half, i.e. a decrease of 37 per cent.[22] Here, too, the effect of more sanitary living conditions is evident.

Malnutrition (the inadequate daily intake of essential foods) occurs mainly in families with low incomes, and is aggravated in the case of Africans by ignorance of correct infant feeding. It is evident in a severe form in the protein deficiency disease known as 'kwashiorkor'. A survey conducted in 1964 showed that 87 per cent of the children affected by this disease were under 4 years of age.[23] There has, however, been a significant diminution of the incidence of severe malnutrition, deaths among city African children under 5 years of age at King Edward VIII Hospital falling from 109 in 1961 to 19 in 1967.[24]

Table 5.2 shows that there has also been a decline of over 50 per cent in the African infant mortality rate during the 1960s. This trend, however, started much earlier as can be gauged from the fact that it was 497,14 per 1 000 live births in 1938, 397,54 in 1942, and 330,02 in 1950; ' . . . child clinics, better housing, basic sanitation and nutrition . . . are obviously having a marked effect on the expectancy of life'.[25] However, the table also shows that there is still a marked difference between the infant mortality rates of Whites and Africans. The reasons for this are probably very varied, but the differences are large enough and the matter important enough to justify a special investigation.

Table 5.2

INFANT MORTALITY RATES PER 1 000 LIVE BIRTHS OF WHITES AND AFRICANS IN DURBAN, 1961–9

Year	Whites	Africans[a]
1961	20,34	167,10
1962	27,23	148,20
1963	24,31	108,63
1964	24,64	104,60
1965	25,99	116,67
1966	25,44	107,18
1967	18,33	111,43
1968	19,55	107,43
1969	14,22	103,39

Source: Annual Reports of the City Medical Officer of Health, 1961–9.
Note: (a)   In 1969 the African infant mortality rate was approximately twice that of Indians, which in turn was twice that of Coloureds.

In addition to King Edward VIII Hospital, general hospital services for Africans are provided by the Mission Hospital at Umlazi and the McCord Zulu Hospital in Durban. Clinics are located either at these hospitals or in the townships. However, there is no clinic at Umlazi and medical expenses are particularly high for its residents; the ambulance fee to King Edward VIII is R6 and the minimum inclusive hospitalization fee is R2 per day.

The proposed decentralization of King Edward VIII Hospital by the building of hospitals at Umlazi and KwaMashu will undoubtedly provide an additional 'on-the-spot' amenity in the townships. However, this can be regarded as an additional amenity only if sufficient hospital facilities remain in the centre of Durban to serve the large African population in daily employment in the central city, as well as those actually residing in the central area.

Hospital statistics may indicate the general state of health of the population, but not necessarily so. The diminution over the years in the death-rate from particular causes may be the result of improved drugs and hospital techniques. However, there is convincing support for the impressions of the Medical Officer of Health quoted above in the comprehensive programmes of health education aimed at the promotion of preventative measures. These programmes include the provision of child clinics, film shows, group discussions and domiciliary visits.

The part played by the various welfare organizations and agencies in the health of Africans in the townships constitutes a vital supplement to their daily budget. In the field in which these organizations work there is no clear demarcation between health and welfare. The major part of the effort is the feeding of children by way of powdered and fresh milk, the cost of which is met by public donations, contributions from the Bantu Revenue Account and a subsidy from the government towards the cost of dried skimmed milk distributed at the child health clinics.

One of the difficulties experienced among families in the townships is that of buying vegetables in the cheapest markets. To overcome this difficulty, groups of women club together and make regular purchases at the municipal market, the local authority providing the necessary transport from the market. A somewhat similar service is provided by Kupugani (a voluntary organization) which specializes in buying fruit and vegetables when there is a glut on the market and then making them available at cost. The relevant marketing boards have supplied potatoes and oranges to the townships, the former at about half the normal retail price and the latter free, the necessary transport and also storage for the potatoes being provided by the municipality.

WELFARE

The major part of welfare work in the municipal area is conducted by the local authority's Bantu Welfare Department and by the Durban Bantu Child Welfare Society. The latter controls and supervises thirteen of the eighteen crèches[26] in the municipal area. There is a great need for crèches as often both parents work; in KwaMashu, for example, the six crèches can accommodate only 560 of the estimated 15 000 children.

The Welfare Department has a substantial income (one-third of the surplus on the Beer Account). It provides a wide range of counselling services and in many cases it is also found necessary to give financial assistance, for example, by way of rent remission.

A serious attempt is being made to assist young Africans with some educational qualifications to find employment, other than domestic service and the more menial forms of labour, by providing general pretraining. Known as the Bantu Youth Employment Scheme, a start was made in 1963 at centres in KwaMashu and Lamont with an initial enrolment of 150.[27] The aim of the trained personnel is to effect a disciplined orientation to work in industry and commerce. Social workers are active in seeking placements to suit the ability of the individual aspirants, with a follow-up system as a check.

South Africa's first out-patient clinic for African alcoholics was opened in KwaMashu in 1969, and additional welfare services include a home for aged and a child welfare home, both at Lamont.

RECREATION

The Welfare Department also takes the initiative in the provision of recreational facilities and is responsible for all relevant planning, building and maintenance in the former municipal townships.

In its townships and hostels the local authority has provided 15 football fields, 3 football stadia, 15 tennis courts, 3 swimming-baths, a bowling green, a cycling track, 3 basketball pitches and 10 community halls. In addition there are 4 junior football fields and a *ngoma* (traditional) dancing-area and a cinema (opened in 1972) at Kwa-Mashu. Additional tennis courts and a swimming-pool are planned for KwaMashu and a YMCA centre is to be opened there. A small section of Durban's beach is reserved for Africans, the training of lifesavers being undertaken by the Welfare Department. A similar range of facilities to those outlined above, but fewer of each, are provided by the state in Umlazi, the only additional facility being a golf-course. There is no athletic track for Africans.

There are no parks in the townships and community leaders regard the halls as inadequate in relation to the demands made upon them. Chesterville is the only township with a library, and the absence of electricity in the larger townships discourages reading in the evenings. All townships have beerhalls, most of which seat 300–600 persons. The lack of public transport within the townships in the evenings and the poor street lighting discourage cinema attendance, but steps are being taken to improve the internal bus services at night.

These facilities are totally inadequate to cater for the needs of the community.[28] Sports facilities in the local authority townships are provided out of beer profits, and no assistance has been given by the government. Recreational facilities provided for Black communities in South Africa are greatly inferior, both in quality and quantity, to those available to Whites.[29] In addition to generous facilities provided by local authorities, the White community has access to far superior school recreational facilities and to a wide range of privately provided facilities. In a society exhibiting large income differentials the allocation of public resources becomes of great significance, and it is clear that the local authority in Durban has failed in this respect, as indeed has the state in its planning of facilities in Umlazi.

OTHER

Both KwaMashu and Umlazi have been planned on the basis of neighbourhood units. These units are self-contained, possessing small shopping centres, churches, schools and playgrounds. All the units connect with a major spiral road (see Map 5). In KwaMashu there is a township centre containing the administration building and offices. The remaining townships all possess roughly similar facilities. In Umlazi a commercial centre is being developed and will include cinemas, apartments, a library and an hotel.

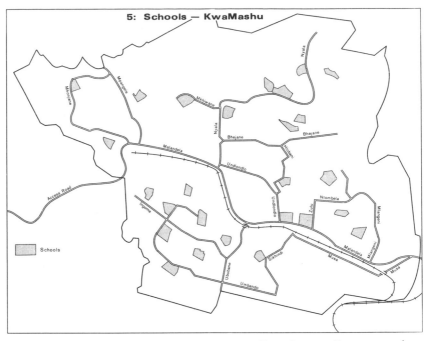

5: Schools — KwaMashu

The shops in the townships are essentially of a small supermarket and general dealer's variety together with a few specialists such as butchers. Many of these enterprises are owned by men who previously operated in the informal sector at Cato Manor. In the new townships the informal sector has less scope to operate because the planned layout allows the authorities a greater measure of control over unlicensed activities. Nevertheless, *shebeens* still exist and are encouraged by the fact that, after the municipal beerhalls and bars close at 5.30 p.m. and 8.30 p.m. respectively, there is a dearth of evening entertainment facilities.[30] Thus the *shebeen* is still fulfilling its traditional role in township life; however, the liquor is purchased from the municipality and illegal brewing and distilling have declined significantly among the resettled communities.

EDUCATION

African education falls under the central government (the Department of Bantu Education). However, local authorities are responsible for the provision of lower and higher primary schools and the maintenance of all schools. The cost of buildings is financed by the government which makes advances from housing funds at economic rates of interest. The instrument by which the local authority finances its obligations is the Bantu Schools Maintenance Account, which derives its income from a monthly levy of 20 cents added to the site rental. The account is chargeable with interest and redemption and maintenance costs. In 1969–70 income totalled R46 000; sewerage charges, repairs and maintenance, water and refuse removals accounted for R28 000 of the total expenditure of R45 000, and loan charges (interest and redemption) for R14 000. Table 5.3 shows school enrolment in the townships in 1971.

Table 5.3

DISTRIBUTION OF AFRICAN PUPILS IN DURBAN AND UMLAZI BY CATEGORY OF SCHOOL,
31 MARCH 1971

Category of school	Umlazi	Kwa-Mashu	Lamont	Chester-ville	Total	
					Number	%
Lower Primary (Sub-Std A–Std 2)	14 315	10 822	2 134	1 061	28 332	55,3
Higher Primary (Std 3–Std 6)	8 201	6 351	1 810	869	17 231	33,6
Secondary and High (Form 1–Form V)	3 095	1 356	507	270	5 228	10,2
Vocational	442	—	—	—	442	0,9
Total	26 053	18 529	4 451	2 200	51 233	100,0

The total enrolment represents 19,5 per cent of the population officially living in family units in the four townships.[31] There are no statistics relating to the number of children of school-going age, but it has been assessed that the 7–14 years age group comprises 25,7 per cent of the family population.[32] Working on a total family population of 256 100 (Table 4.2), we arrive at some 65 700 of primary school age. The actual primary school enrolment of 41 400 represents 63 per cent of this figure. A further analysis indicates that the proportion of the relevant age groups actually at school is significantly higher in the lower than in the higher primary schools.

The distribution of pupils by standard of the different race groups in metropolitan Durban affords an interesting comparison.[33] In White schools the first four standards (including substandards) comprise 38,5 per cent of enrolment, the second four 36,4 per cent and the last four 25,1 per cent. The corresponding percentages of African enrolment in 1971 were 55,8, 33,9 and 10,3; this disparity emphasizes the high drop-out rate and the consequent paucity of numbers in African secondary and high schools.

Post-primary education in the Durban area is represented by seven secondary schools, three high schools (two in Umlazi and one in KwaMashu) and one vocational training school, together comprising 11,1 per cent of the school population. Secondary schools proceed to Form III only, the Junior Certificate level; pupils wishing to con-

tinue to Form V (Standard X or Matriculation level) have to attend
one of the high schools.

Lamont and Chesterville are served by one secondary school each,
and pupils from these areas attend high school in Umlazi. One of the
high schools in Umlazi has a hostel to accommodate pupils from other
areas. There is one secondary school and one high school at KwaMashu
while Umlazi has four secondary and two high schools as well as a
vocational training school which provides instruction in a wide range
of subjects. Nine night schools function in the area—seven at Umlazi
and one each at Lamont and KwaMashu. The total night school
enrolment is approximately 1 300, of whom 17 per cent are females.
The location of schools in relation to the main arterial routes in
KwaMashu is shown in Map 5.

As there is no statutory compulsion for African children to attend
school, there is no machinery for enforcing attendance by enrolled
pupils. Another factor affecting enrolment is economic pressure—the
rising cost of keeping a child at school as he progresses through the
standards, and the need to supplement family income by sending the
young son to work. Many daughters leave school early so that they
can tend the home and younger children. However, school registers
show an average attendance (that is attendance to enrolment) of 98
per cent in 1971.

Generally these factors appear to affect boys more than girls. In the
substandards boys constitute over 50 per cent of the pupils; this
proportion falls to less than 45 per cent in Standard 6 but in Forms IV
and V increases to over 60 per cent, perhaps because of the more
serious objective of a career.

CONCLUSION

Although they offer improved physical standards of housing, most
rehousing estates in cities, whether in developed or less developed
countries, tend to be characterized by drabness and uniformity. Thus,
Hance has written of African townships in South African cities: 'While
monotonous in the extreme, there is no doubt that they provide
distinctly superior facilities to the notorious slums and shanty towns
they replaced'.[34]

Durban's new townships are certainly monotonous, but given the
favourable climate their streets will in time be lined with trees and
their gardens filled with banana and mango trees and subtropical
plants as in the older townships of Lamont and Chesterville (in this
respect Durban is more fortunate than the bleak townships of the
Transvaal Highveld). The standard of housing represents a substantial
improvement on Cato Manor. But the residents find that life in the
townships lacks the gaiety and spontaneity of Cato Manor although
the townships are gradually developing a character of their own.[35]
Writing of the cities of colonial Africa Blair states that too often Africans

felt no sense of civic identity; their social and cultural requirements were inadequately provided for and the cities were merely administrative areas 'incidentally inhabited by Africans'.[36] Similar views have been expressed by some Africans about the townships in South Africa.[37]

More importantly, however, they are still centres of poverty in juxtaposition to cities and suburbs of great affluence, and it is to an analysis and discussion of this phenomenon that we now turn our attention.

NOTES AND REFERENCES

1 A more detailed descriptive account is contained in a paper being prepared for publication by P. A. Ellison, Department of Economics, University of Natal.

2 The Deputy Minister of Bantu Administration and Development has stated that only men who subscribe to National Party policy will be appointed as chairmen of boards. *Daily News*, 7 May 1973.

3 For a summary of the debates see Muriel Horrell, *A Survey of Race Relations in South Africa* (annual), Johannesburg: South African Institute of Race Relations, 1969, p. 145 et seq. and 1971, p. 132 et seq.

4 A statutory account required by the Bantu (Urban Areas) Consolidation Account No. 25 of 1945.

5 All figures relating to the account are taken from the *City Treasurer's Report and Abstract Accounts, year ended 31 July 1970*.

6 However, a small increase of 10 per cent is envisaged for the next two years, after which rentals will be reviewed.

7 The inspectorate checks that all African employees are registered and that all service levy fees are paid. It is also responsible for shack demolitions and controls illegal shack erections.

8 Horrell, op. cit., 1971, p. 139.

9 *Durban Housing Survey*, op. cit., pp. 304–5.

10 Hellman, op. cit., p. 5.

11 Horrell, op. cit., 1971, p. 139.

12 See Harry W. Richardson, *Regional Economics*, London: Weidenfeld and Nicolson, 1969, pp. 189–92.

13 Ibid.

14 Muriel Horrell, *A Survey of Race Relations in South Africa*, 1972, Johannesburg: South African Institute of Race Relations, p. 142.

15 Ibid., p. 144.

16 In addition to the accounts in Table 6:1 there are three specified trust accounts operated by the Durban Corporation, viz. the Bantu Services Levy Fund, the Bantu Transport Levy Fund and the Bantu Schools Maintenance Account.

17 City of Durban, *Annual Report of the Medical Officer of Health*, 1967, p. 127.

18 Certain employers provide transport, particularly those who find it essential to get the team of workers together at a place relatively inaccessible to bus or train, e.g. builders.

19 The proportion of African to Indian patients is reported to be 16:1. See H. L. Watts & N. K. Lamond, *A Study of the Social Circumstances and Characteristics of the Bantu in the Durban Region*, Report No. 2; Durban: Institute for Social Research, University of Natal, 1966, p. 45.

20 City of Durban, *Annual Report of the Medical Officer of Health*, 1969.

21 Ibid.

22 Ibid.

23 Watts & Lamond, op. cit., p. 31.

24 City of Durban, *Annual Report of the Medical Officer of Health*, 1969.

25 City of Durban, *Annual Report of the Medical Officer of Health*, 1961, p. 4.

26 This term is used broadly to cover nursery schools, crèches and playgroups. The crèches in the townships operate to some extent like nursery schools.

27 Present enrolment is about half this number; no particular reason has been advanced for this decrease.

28 In one township children are permitted to use the swimming-pool for only 30 minutes at a time during the summer holidays because of the great demand.

29 The Coloured and Indian communities of Durban also suffer from inadequate recreational facilities; these are provided by the Corporation out of Borough Funds and provide a good illustration of the failure of local authorities in South Africa to fulfil the allocative and distributive budget functions.

30 In Umlazi, however, the beerhalls close at 10 p.m.

31 The family population is based on Table 4.2.

32 P. A. Nel, M. Loubser & J. J. A. Steenekamp, *Income and Expenditure Patterns of Non-White Urban Households—Durban Survey*, Pretoria: University of South Africa Bureau of Market Research, 1971, Table 3.1.

33 H. L. Watts, *Urbanisation and Education in Durban*, Durban: South African Institute of Race Relations, No. 7/70, Table 1.

34 Hance, op. cit., p. 288. Although Hance's views of housing conflict with the evidence on informal sector housing discussed in chapter 4, the public services in the townships are generally superior to those in the old shack areas.

35 For similar observations elsewhere in Africa see Marris, *Family and Social Change . . .*, op. cit., p. 123. For a good description of the vibrant life in Sophiatown and other African areas of Johannesburg, and expressions of regret at their demolition, see Can Themba, *The Will to Die*, African Writers Series No. 104, London: Heinemann, 1971.

36 Blair, op. cit., p. 229.

37 Umlazi now has an elected Town Council and KwaMashu an Urban Bantu Council, and greater public participation in the process of local government may result in a change in these attitudes.

CHAPTER 6

Economic Growth and the Urban African

The period since the new townships of Durban were opened has, in the main, been characterized by a rapid rate of economic growth in South Africa; during the 1960s the economy showed one of the highest growth rates in the world. The purpose of this chapter is to discern the extent to which the Durban African community shared in this growth. Has the real income of households increased and has the incidence of poverty diminished? These are questions which can only be answered in the broader framework of the concept of poverty as it has been applied in South Africa and of the distribution of income.

AFRICAN INCOMES, 1958–9 TO 1970–1

In 1964–5 and again in 1970–1 the Bureau of Market Research (BMR) of the University of South Africa undertook surveys of Durban African households.[1] The aim of their surveys, as market reaserch projects, differed from that of our 1959 study (chapter 2) so that their use for comparative purposes is limited. Another important factor to bear in mind is that scientific sampling was not feasible in the 1959 study, as explained in chapter 2. However, the three surveys do provide some indication of trends between 1959 and 1971.

We shall first compare our 1959 family budget study with the earlier BMR study. The main difficulties in comparing the results of the surveys are changes in price levels and the use of different income intervals. The former can be corrected approximately by a consumer price index adjustment, viz. a rise of 16 per cent in the index over the six year period.[2] The latter difficulty may be overcome by finding equal or near equal points in the income groups in the two surveys. In this way changes in real income can be illustrated.

In 1959, 69 per cent of households had weekly incomes of less than R8,50 (or R36,83 per month) and 58 per cent weekly incomes of less than R7,50 (or R32,50 per month). These figures are equivalent to R42,72 and R37,80 per month respectively in 1964–5. The 1964–5 BMR survey shows that only 30 per cent of households (or approximately one-half of the proportion in 1959) had incomes of under R40 per month.[3] It also shows that 79 per cent of households had an income of under R80 per month, whereas the earlier study showed that 95–97 per cent of households had a monthly income of less than R80 (calculated and adjusted on the same basis as in the previous example). Thus there was a significant increase of 55 per cent in the mean real income of households during the period. Real *per capita* income increased by 41 per cent, the difference between these figures being accounted for by the increase in mean family size from 4,9 to 5,4 persons.

Both surveys give a median monthly household income, the 1959 figure being R30,30 and the 1964–5 figure R52,82.[4] If the earlier figure is adjusted by the consumer price index it becomes R35,15. There was thus an increase in the median household income of 50 per cent during the period. This trend appears to have been nationwide; for example, during the period 1960–4 there was an increase of 32 per cent in the median African household income in Pretoria.[5]

A comparison of the two surveys reveals that the masculinity rate increased from 90 to 91,2, wage-earners as a proportion of the population from 25,5 per cent to 28,8 per cent, females as a proportion of wage-earners from 17 per cent to 29 per cent, and the average number of earners per household from 1,26 to 1,55. Though some increase in the masculinity rate is noted, it is the significant increase in the proportion of female earners which would largely account for the increase in the proportion of workers in the population and the average number of earners per household.

There is a marked difference in economic conditions in the two survey years. It can perhaps be assumed that there has always been a 'push' stress on the African household to increase its number of workers. It is possible that with the improved economic conditions in 1964–5 women were encouraged to seek work by a firmer demand for their labour. An increase in the number of earners in the household will, of course, enhance the household income, and an increase in wages will have the same effect. Unfortunately, comparative wages are not available in the two reports.

An analysis of average monthly household expenditure (Table 6.1)

Table 6.1

DISTRIBUTION OF AVERAGE MONTHLY HOUSEHOLD EXPENDITURE 1959 AND 1964–65.

Item	1959			1964–5	
	Actual R	Adjusted by Price Index R	%	Actual R	%
Food	33,37	38,71	53,1	28,63	42,5
Rent	4,33	5,02	6,9	5,68	8,4
Other PDL components	13,87	16,09	22,1	16,77	24,9
Non-PDL components	11,27	13,07	17,9	16,32	24,2
Total	62,84	72,89	100,0	67,40	100,0

Sources: 1959 Survey; BMR Report 1964–5, Table XXXVI.

reveals a decrease in real terms of 7,5 per cent. This gives *per capita* expenditures of R14,88 and R12,48 in the respective years, a decrease of 16,6 per cent.

In 1959 the mean household weekly wage income was R7,70. If this is raised by 3 per cent to obtain mean total household income[6] the resultant figure of R7,93 represents 54,7 per cent of the mean household expenditure of R14,50. The BMR survey showed a mean household income of R59,84 per month, which represents 88,8 per cent of the mean household expenditure of R67,40.[7] These percentages indicate that disclosed income made a larger contribution towards meeting expenditure in the later survey. The reasons for this disparity can only be a matter of conjecture. Apart from the survey problems of maintaining the validity of the random sample and of obtaining reliable information from respondents, there might have been a difference in the degree of co-operation received in the two surveys. An important factor which we have already noted is that in the new townships opportunities for supplementary sources of income via the informal sector have become more limited. Perhaps the general increase in real income has reduced the necessity of finding supplementary sources of income. On the other hand we have noted that there may have been a tendency to overstate expenditure in the 1959 study.

There was a marked disparity in *per capita* expenditure on food which fell from R7,49 in 1959 to R5,02 in 1964–5, a decrease of 33 per cent. This decrease may have been due to the increased cost of unavoidable items such as rent, transport, and fuel and light following resettlement in the new townships.

However, part of the decrease may be accounted for by an increase in various forms of subsidized feeding and food schemes.[8] It is possible that in the case of children at school parents may have included any contributions they made to school-feeding schemes in their assessment of expenditure on education. There may also have been an increasing trend for employers to pay wages in kind (including food). This would have had the effect of reducing the family expenditure on food. The increase in the proportion of economically active women would also enhance such a trend.[9] Many domestic employees, apart from receiving food as part of their earnings, take home food contributed either voluntarily or involuntarily by their employers.

A comparison of the two BMR surveys reveals that the real income of urban African households in the Durban area increased further during the second half of the 1960s. A survey conducted by the BMR between September 1970 and February 1971 found an average annual household income of R932,86.[10] In this survey 84 adult children, who retained more than R10 of their monthly income for their own use, were not regarded as members of their households. Their inclusion, which is relevant for our purposes, would have the effect of increasing the average income to R1 046,40.[11]

In the period between the two BMR surveys, the consumer price index for Africans, as computed in this study, rose by 37,2 per cent. Using this figure to adjust the income of R1 046,40 to the 1964–5 level gives a real average monthly household income of R63,56. This represents an increase in real income between 1964–5 and 1970–1 of 6,2 per cent. This differs somewhat from the position in Cape Town where the estimated increase of 20 per cent in African real income during the 1960s was apparently gained during the early years of the decade; 'between 1964–5 and 1970 there may well have been a fall of real income'.[12] Much political significance has been attributed to the fact that African real incomes have increased, and according to Adam the relative improvement in their economic situation takes the sting out of their deprivation.[13]

The tendency for the proportion of workers to increase continued during this period, the proportion rising from 28,8 per cent in 1964–5 to 33,3 per cent in 1970–1.[14] This can be attributed largely to the continuing increase in the proportion of female earners; the sex of the 84 adult children workers was not specified in the report but the proportion of female workers was between 36 and 48 per cent compared with 29 per cent in 1964–5.[15] The average of 1,84 earners per household[16] represents a substantial increase on the 1964–5 figure of 1,55.

A comparison of mean *per capita* monthly incomes in the two surveys, again using a consumer price adjustment, gives an average *per capita* real income of R11,18 in 1970–1 compared with R11,12 for 1964–5. Thus the increase in *per capita* real income was only marginal during the second half of the 1960s.

Wage income constituted approximately 93 per cent of total household disclosed income in 1959, 86 per cent in 1964–5 and 84 per cent in 1970–1.[17] The balance of income comprised such items as proprietors' earnings (business, property and investments), income from subletting, pensions, gifts and disclosed illegal and other informal earnings. The decline in the relative importance of wage incomes is probably explained by the increase in the number of African proprietors conducting licensed businesses. Thus the proportion of income accruing by way of proprietors' earnings, which was negligible in 1959 (when most of the supplementary income was derived from subletting) was 6,3 per cent in 1964–5 and 7 per cent in 1970–1.[18]

In 1970–1, mean household income was 94,4 per cent of mean household expenditure,[19] appreciably larger than the figure of 88,8 per cent in 1964–5. Table 6.2 shows a further reduction in the percentage of expenditure on food during this period (cf. Table 6.1). It is interesting to note that expenditure on non-PDL components (29,9 per cent) is the same as that found among Indians in Durban in 1965,[20] and that it also corresponds closely, if an allowance for non-essential transport is added, to the one-third found by Batson in his estimate of the EML.[21]

Table 6.2

DISTRIBUTION OF AVERAGE MONTHLY HOUSEHOLD EXPENDITURE, 1970–1

Item	Actual (R)	Deflated to 1964 price level (R)	%
Food	32,64	27,66	39,6
Rent	5,83	4,94	7,1
Other PDL components (a)	19,30	16,35	23,4
Non-PDL components	24,61	20,86	29,9
Total	82,38	69,81	100,0

Source: BMR Report 1970–1, Table 3.21(a).

Note: (a) All household transport is included as no distinction is made in the two surveys between the essential transport costs of earners and other expenditure on transport.

THE MEAN POVERTY DATUM LINE, 1971[22]

In March 1972 we undertook fieldwork in order to update the costs of PDL items for Africans. Concurrently we collected identical data for March 1971 to enable us to compile a PDL which would provide a near basis of comparison with the 1970–1 BMR report. We found that it was easy to obtain accurate data for 1971; not only were the records of shopkeepers available for scrutiny but the shopkeepers and their assistants kept a close check on price movements and were able to recall the prices ruling twelve months earlier.

There is no such thing as *the* PDL. In any community the PDL will vary from one household to another, depending on the size of the household, the age and sex structure, and the activity of its members. However, in order to convey some idea of an average figure, PDLs have usually been calculated for a hypothetical family of five or six persons, which approaches the median or mean-sized household in most African communities. The composition of such a hypothetical family is entirely arbitrary, and this is clearly an unsatisfactory base for a PDL calculation. We decided, therefore, to introduce a new method, viz. that of a mean rather than a hypothetical PDL, which we believe to be less subjective and arbitrary than previous methods.

The 1970–1 BMR survey provided the demographic data required for our purposes. In our analysis we utilized data relating to 314 households out of the BMR sample of 361 households. Single-person households were excluded as being irrelevant in a study concerned with families, and the small group of households of ten persons and over, being open-ended, was also excluded. It was felt that these omissions largely compensated each other.

This information enabled us to analyse the total sample by age, sex, activity and number of earners. By taking into account all these variables in their correct proportions we obtained a *weighted mean* household of 5,2 persons.[23] This mean-sized household cannot itself be broken down into age, sex and activity components. The PDL for this weighted mean household, or in other words the mean PDL, is shown in Table 6.3.

Table 6.3

MEAN POVERTY DATUM LINE AND EFFECTIVE MINIMUM LEVEL, MARCH 1971

Component	R
Food	43,95
Clothing	7,96
Cleansing	2,35
Fuel and lighting	1,66
Accommodation	6,72
Transport	4,56
Taxation	0,67
PDL	67,87
PDL excluding tax	67,20
Add 50%	33,60
Taxation	1,37
EML	102,17

In compiling the PDL costs the same components and quantities of food, clothing, fuel and light, and cleansing materials were used as in 1958–9, while in the case of clothing the same durability of the components was adhered to. Fieldwork involved the close observation of African customers in shops, both in the city itself and in KwaMashu.

The same accommodation cost of R6,72 has been allocated for all households. This is based on the rent of four-roomed houses in Kwa-Mashu[24] and Umlazi, after adding 51 cents for water for KwaMashu where it is metered.[25] There is a relatively small variation in the rents of detached and semi-detached houses in KwaMashu, the mean rent being R6,57 after making the above adjustments. In Umlazi the relatively small variation in rents depends on the size of the plot; here the mean figure is R6,87. These net figures give the average of R6,72 used in the table.[26]

The final constituent item of the PDL is direct taxation which amounted to 67 cents—46 cents on a monthly income of R67,20 and 21 cents in respect of the fixed annual tax of R2,50 on all African males over 17 years of age. This gave a mean total PDL cost of R67,87. Taxation is 70 cents more in the case of the EML, giving a mean total EML cost of R102,17 per month. This figure fell within the R83–104 monthly income group in the BMR report. Overall, 91 per cent of the earners received less than R83 and 95 per cent less than R104 per month. Thus only approximately 4–9 per cent of earners received incomes in excess of the EML.

The level of household income is, of course, affected by the number of earners in the household. The households with only one earner (51,1 per cent) had an average monthly income of R63,01, those with two earners (comprising 40,7 per cent of households) had an average monthly income of R88,05, and those with three, four and five-plus earners had monthly incomes of R107,52, R112,74 and R197,60 respectively.[27]

Thus family incomes are by no means proportional to the number of earners in the household, and this has an important implication. The position can be seen more clearly when average incomes are compared by types of earners. The average earnings of household heads was R60,90, of wives R27,72 and of 'others' R30,71.[28] The weighted average of the two latter groups is R28,78, or less than half the income of the head of household. There are on average 1,6 earners per household, but it is obviously incorrect to deduce that the average family income is R60,90 × 1,6. It is more likely to approximate R60,90 × 1,3, that is about R79.[29] The average income shown by the survey is in fact about R78.

The effect of the increase in the number of earners per household with family size is illustrated in Table 6.4. About 96 per cent of households fell within the first two income groups; 78,8 per cent of households with one to three persons had an income below R83, and the percentage in this income group shows a progressive decrease as the size of household increases. There is a correspondingly progressive increase in the percentage of households in the higher income groups as the size of household increases.

The cumulative percentages in Table 6.5 suggest that approximately 50–55 per cent of households received incomes below the mean PDL

Table 6.4

DISTRIBUTION OF HOUSEHOLDS BY SIZE AND MONTHLY INCOME GROUPS, 1970–1

Income group (R)	Household size				
	1–3	4–6	7–9	10 +	Total
0– 83,33	78,8	66,2	63,8	55,2	68,1
83,34–166,66	20,2	29,6	31,8	37,9	28,3
166,67–249,99	1,0	2,8	4,4	6,9	3,0
250,00 +	—	1,4	—	—	0,6
Total (= 100%)	99	142	91	29	361

Source: BMR Report 1970–1, Table 3.20(c)

of R67,87 per month. This represents an improvement over the position in 1958 when the survey in Cato Manor showed that 66 per cent of households were below their PDL. The table also shows that the income of 68 per cent of households was less than R83 and that 84,1 per cent had an income of less than R104; the preponderance of households in the lower income groups suggests that about 80 per cent of households had an income under the EML of R102,17 per month.

Table 6.5

PERCENTAGE DISTRIBUTION OF HOUSEHOLDS BY INCOME GROUP

Monthly income group (R)	Households	
	%	Cumulative %
0– 20,82	3,3	3,3
20,84– 41,66	10,2	13,5
41,67– 62,49	30,7	44,2
62,50– 83,33	23,8	68,0
83,34–104,16	16,1	84,1
104,17–124,99	4,7	88,8
125,00–145,83	3,9	92,7
145,84–166,66	3,6	96,3
166,67–187,49	1,4	97,7
187,50–208,33	1,1	98,8
208,34–249,99	0,6	99,4
250,00–333,33	0,3	99,7
333,34+	0,3	100,0
Total No. (=100%)	361	

Source: BMR Report 1970–1, Table 3.17.

THE EFFECTIVE MINIMUM LEVEL

The technical base of any attempt to arrive at the EML is the Poverty Datum Line (PDL). The common element of all the components of the PDL (outlined in chapter 1) is that they are recurrent items of expenditure affecting all households.

The PDL does not include all items of household expenditure which may be regarded as essential, e.g. medical and education expenses, but such items do not possess this common element. Apart from such obvious essentials, households at all levels of income make disbursements on such items as furniture, tobacco, recreation, personal care and religious expenses, often to the detriment of expenditure on basic needs such as food. The calculation of the EML, for which the PDL is the technical base, is an attempt to take these additional items of expenditure into account. These items are henceforth referred to as extra-PDL items.

We have noted (p. 19) that the EML is commonly assumed to be 150 per cent of the PDL, following the results of Batson's early studies of expenditure patterns. We have attempted to test the validity of this figure by reference to the two BMR surveys. In the case of the 1964–5 study we assessed the PDL (R58,75) as the mean of costs obtained from studies conducted in 1964 and 1966,[30] while the food cost (R33,12) was assessed on the basis of the latter study adjusted by the consumer price index. In the case of the 1970–1 study we applied our 1971 PDL figures.

These PDL and food costs were then compared with expenditure. In considering expenditure on extra-PDL items we made allowance for both the inclusion and the exclusion of insurance and savings. This is because it is difficult to determine whether these items constitute a surplus of income or not. Though on the face of it they may appear to be a surplus, it is possible that some households regard them as a priority charge on their extra-PDL expenditure.

It is reasonable to assume that the extent of extra-PDL expenditure acceptable for an EML assessment is found at that minimum level of income where expenditure on all PDL items in general and on food in particular covers their assessed costs. In 1964–5 PDL and food costs were covered at the same income level; at this level expenditure on extra-PDL items amounted to 43,1 per cent of the PDL if insurance and savings are included, and 42,2 per cent if they are excluded. In 1970–1, expenditure on all PDL items covered PDL costs at an income level at which the comparable percentages were 63,5 and 55,7. However expenditure on food covered PDL food costs at a higher income level.

Food is the major component of the PDL and also of actual expenditure on PDL items. In 1964–5 and 1970–1 food accounted for 56,4 per cent and 65,4 per cent respectively of PDL costs, the overall proportions of actual expenditure being approximately 58 per cent in both cases. But expenditure on food does not necessarily account for all the food consumed, and discrepancies not taken into account in most studies may be categorized as follows:

(i) Free: meals supplied in industry, commerce and domestic service; free feeding schemes in the townships; free hand-outs of oranges.

(ii) Subsidized: meals supplied at subeconomic rates in canteens; various infant- and school-feeding schemes in the townships; potato distribution in the townships.

(iii) Economic rates in canteens: the deduction is not disclosed by the respondent as part of his household expenditure on food.

(iv) The food value of traditional beer.

The above factors, if they could be taken into account, would mean that expenditure on food would tend to equate to food cost at lower levels of income than those shown in our investigation.[31] Therefore, in order to determine the level of income that would indicate an EML, it would appear more practical to use the income groups which cover PDL costs rather than those covering food costs. This would in any case have the advantage of ensuring a conservative estimate; for this reason expenditure on insurance and savings should also be excluded. On this basis, the tables, taken together, show that in the lowest income groups where actual expenditure on total PDL components covers assessed PDL costs, expenditure on extra-PDL items ranges from 42,2 per cent to 55,7 per cent of PDL costs.

The foregoing indicates the difficulties in establishing even an approximate percentage that should be added to the PDL to arrive at an EML. In the first instance one must be sure of the accuracy of the PDL base. The use of a hypothetical family to assess the PDL does not take these variables into account, thus giving an unreliable basis for any EML assessment. Further, expenditure patterns change and also vary between different social and race groups. There is also the question of what items of expenditure if any should be excluded from such an assessment; reference to this has already been made in the case of insurance and savings.

The concept of an approximate EML percentage which can be generally applied is based on the assumption that PDL components (taken together) and extra-PDL items (taken together) are subject to the same price changes. However, if the increase in the price of the former is greater than that of the latter, the EML percentage will decrease. Conversely, if the increase in the price of the former is smaller, then the EML percentage will increase. This has an important implication in the case of resettled communities, where the accommodation component of the PDL has been subject to little change. This would account to some extent for the significant differences in the relationship between extra-PDL expenditure and PDL costs, viz. 42,2 per cent in 1964–5 and 55,7 per cent in 1970–1.

The conclusion drawn is that it is not possible to give an accurate EML percentage even at a particular time, and that if this were possible, it would have only short-term value for a particular group of people. However, for practical purposes it would appear that, on the basis of available data, 50 per cent could be regarded as an acceptable minimum to be added to the PDL in order to obtain the EML, thus verifying Batson's original figure.

PRICE CHANGES 1959–71

The following section attempts to analyse and assess the effect of changes in prices between the years 1959 and 1971 on the African household budget.

Table 6.6 shows assessed PDL costs in the two years. Data from the 1970–1 BMR report are used to ensure that the categorized households are fully representative of age and sex distribution, number and type of earners and degree of activity. These factors are assumed to be the same for the 1959 families, an assumption considered to be justified for the purpose of the table, which is to compare costs in the two years.

Table 6.6

COMPARISON OF PDL COSTS, 1959–71

Size of household (persons)	Total PDL Costs		Increase 1959–71	
	1959	1971	R	%
2	21,05	32,52	11,47	54
3	28,54	45,78	17,24	60
4	37,47	59,75	22,28	60
5	39,43	63,37	23,94	61
6	44,36	74,52	30,16	68
7	50,09	85,09	35,00	70
8	55,59	94,56	38,93	70
9	61,34	102,61	41,27	67

Source: 1959 Survey; Table 6.3.

The table shows an increase in PDL costs ranging from approximately 60 per cent in the three- to five-person households to approximately 70 per cent in the larger households, giving an arithmetic mean of about 65 per cent. This corresponds approximately to the mean of the increases in the five and six-person households, which represent the average-size family.

Food comprised 65,4 per cent of PDL costs in 1971, clothing 11,8 per cent, cleansing and fuel and light 3,5 per cent each, transport 6,8 per cent and accommodation 10 per cent. During the period 1959–71 accommodation costs increased by 11,6 per cent and transport costs by 10 per cent. Table 6.7 shows the increases in the two largest components of PDL costs, viz. food and clothing.

It is evident that the large increase in food costs, ranging from 78,4 per cent to 87,6 per cent, has been of prime importance in the increase in total PDL costs.

Table 6.7

PERCENTAGE INCREASES IN THE PDL COST OF FOOD AND CLOTHING, 1959–71

Size of household (persons)	Food	Clothing
2	78,5	62,7
3	79,1	62,2
4	78,8	62,4
5	78,4	62,7
6	80,3	64,8
7	87,6	61,0
8	85,4	63,5
9	79,6	61,4

Source: 1959 Survey; Table 6.3.

Table 6.8 is an analysis of actual expenditure in 1970–1. It shows
that expenditure on food averaged 58 per cent of expenditure on total
PDL items; this proportion is approximately the same for all income
groups except the lowest and the highest groups, and is 7,4 per cent
smaller than the relevant proportion based on costs in the table. The
discrepancy may to some extent be accounted for by two broad factors,
viz. the tendency of lower income groups to economize on food, and
food made available by external sources that is additional to food
actually purchased.

Table 6.8

EXPENDITURE ON FOOD AS A PERCENTAGE OF EXPENDITURE ON PDL ITEMS AND OF
TOTAL EXPENDITURE, 1971

Income group (R)	Food expenditure as % of:	
	PDL expenditure	Total expenditure
0– 20,83	66,4	58,7
20,84– 41,66	61,3	51,7
41,67– 62,49	59,9	46,7
62,50– 83,33	58,0	41,7
83,34–104,16	58,0	38,1
104,17–124,99	56,7	34,7
125,00–145,83	61,0	32,7
145,84–166,66	58,2	31,7
166,67+	48,4	21,7
Total	58,0	40,7

Source: Table 6.7.

As a proportion of total expenditure, food outlays averaged 40,7
per cent, with a range of 38,1 to 51,7 per cent in the income groups
from R20 to R104, which accounted for over 80 per cent of the sample.

This proportion of total expenditure devoted to food is considerably
higher than the 24,7 per cent of total consumer expenditure allocated to
food in the weighted consumer price index (CPI) for South Africa.
This is understandable since the CPI is based on a 1966 survey of White
family expenditure and Engel's Law would naturally operate. But it
does illustrate that the CPI is an inadequate indicator by which to
gauge changes in the real income of African families.

Because Africans spend proportionately more of their incomes on
food than do Whites, they are harder hit by rises in food costs. And it is
precisely food prices which tend to rise faster than those of other items.
For example, between 1965 and 1971 the CPI reflected a 21 per cent
increase in the food index compared with 17,2 per cent for furniture
and equipment and 7,1 per cent for clothing.

It is, however, possible to obtain an index of the increases in African household costs from 1959 to 1971 on the basis of actual expenditure. This is done in three steps, viz.

(i) From the following expenditure calculation:

	%	%
Expenditure on PDL items	67,36	
Expenditure on extra-PDL items taken into account	26,68	
		94,04
Expenditure on extra-PDL items not taken into account:		
Insurance	0,62	
Taxes	0,96	
Savings	4,28	
		5,86
		99,90

(ii) Between 1959 and 1971 PDL costs increased by 64,5 per cent (the arithmetic mean of the five to six-person households), while extra PDL costs increased by 45,3 per cent (weighting the official CPI of all extra-PDL items taken into account).

(iii) By combining (i) and (ii) we find the overall index of the increase in household costs:

$$6\ 736 \times 1\ 645 = 11\ 080\ 720$$
$$2\ 668 \times 1\ 453 = \ \ 3\ 876\ 604$$

$$9\ 404 \qquad\qquad 14\ 957\ 324$$

$$14\ 957\ 324 \div 9\ 404 = 159,1$$

This indicates an overall increase in household costs on the basis of actual expenditure from 1959 to 1971 of 59 per cent, as compared with the official consumer price index increase of 32 per cent.

Thus the cost of living for Africans increased at almost double the rate indicated by the CPI. The CPI is based on White family expenditure in the twelve major urban areas of South Africa. As such it is an inaccurate guide to the position of White families in rural areas and it is clearly inapplicable to the position of the Black communities. There is a great need for the construction of a CPI for each race group in a country with such sharp inter-racial income divisions.

POVERTY CONCEPTS—AN EVALUATION OF THE PDL

Many writers have pointed to the shortcomings of subsistence measures of poverty, of which the PDL is one.[32] These shortcomings are both methodological and conceptual. Criticisms on methodological grounds relate mainly to problems of measuring the basic components such as food and clothing.

Whilst the procedures for estimating minimum nutritional requirements have been improved, the estimates will vary from one society to another and accepted international standards are lacking. In the United States, where poverty has been defined as nutritional inadequacy, attempts have been made to define a market basket of food items sufficient to prevent such poverty. The basket is costed so that it is the most economical possible. But Rein points to fundamental deficiencies in such a measure:[33]

(i) It assumes an efficient housekeeper who has the knowledge, skill and mobility to purchase in the most economical way. But in fact the low-income housewife is likely to be a less informed customer.

(ii) Studies have shown that the poor in fact pay more for food since they are unable to exploit the economies of bulk purchase. Stigler pointed out in 1945 that people did not purchase the lowest-cost food items. Thus in costing food requirements it would be more realistic to consider actual consumption patterns.

Our observations confirm that these reservations are indeed pertinent to the local situation.

In a multiracial society the extent to which a PDL should be racially determined is an important question. It is particularly pertinent if cultural differences between the various groups are reflected in their respective eating habits. Thomson and Kay refer to the different food requirements and eating habits of Africans in the then Northern Rhodesia; they show clearly that European-type foods such as bread, tea, sugar and milk become increasingly popular as customs change in an urban environment.[34] In his study in Salisbury Batson attempted to construct one dietary scale for all race groups; similarly, the scale used in our PDL calculations is culturally neutral in that the minimum nutritional requirements laid down are applicable to all groups.

But the use of a common, culturally neutral nutritional table does not imply that differences in eating habits are ignored; on the contrary, it recognizes the existence of such differences. Thus the African cereal diet revolves around maize products while rice and flour, which are more expensive, are used in traditional Indian dishes.

Two nationwide studies undertaken in 1973, by Nel *et al*[35] and Potgieter,[36] used a new food-ration scale originally based on American standards and subsequently adapted by the Department of Health to the eating habits of the various race groups. Nel's study covered Africans, Coloureds and Indians and Potgieter's Africans and Coloureds.

The calorie and protein allowances in this ration scale are significantly lower than in ours. This is in line with the results of continuing research in the nutrition field which has shown that minimum requirements are lower than hitherto believed. But it is when a nutritional table is translated into a ration scale that it becomes controversial, and it is here that we believe the Department of Health's table for Africans suffers from certain shortcomings. Judging both from an analysis of expenditure studies and from our observations, it fails to take sufficient account of the established eating habits of the urban community. For example expenditure surveys reveal a distinct preference on the part of Durban Africans for meat and fresh milk rather than fish and powdered milk, which are allowed for in the food-ration scale. The costing of our PDL has involved a considerable amount of fieldwork, necessitating the close observation of African buying habits at shops in the townships as well as in the city. The PDL food items have been selected so as to meet the minimum nutritional requirements whilst at the same time conforming as closely as possible to actual consumption patterns.

A study of African housing in 1966–7 revealed that only 10 per cent of Durban African families had rural backgrounds and that the average period of urban residence was 14,4 years.[37] It is reasonable to assume, therefore, and this is indeed confirmed by our fieldwork, that traditional customs and eating habits have undergone a substantial change in the Durban metropolitan area.

The Department of Health's food-ration scale for Africans is less generous than our nutritional table and, since food constitutes the bulk of PDL costs, this accounts for the fact that our PDL and EML figures are significantly higher than the comparable figures produced by the other studies.

Potgieter, for example, calculated the PDL for a hypothetical household of six persons at R78,12 in March/April 1973,[38] while our mean PDL for March 1973 was R95,26.[39] The biggest difference between our mean PDL and Potgieter's figure occurs in the food component, our allocation being higher by almost R31. According to the well-known Engel's Law low-income groups spend a larger proportion of their income on food than high-income groups. The BMR study of 1971 revealed that for six-person households 61,6 per cent of expenditure on all PDL items was devoted to food. The PDL assumes the wise allocation of income among all constituent items, but budget studies have shown that at low levels of income households are obliged to economize on food in order to meet other commitments. Thus one would in fact expect food to constitute more than 61,6 per cent of PDL costs. This expectation is met in our results which showed that in March 1971 food accounted for 65,4 per cent, and in March 1973 for 73,5 per cent, of total PDL costs. In contrast, food constitutes only 49 per cent of Potgieter's PDL costs.

The purpose of Nel's study was not to assess poverty but rather to assist in minimum-wage setting. This was done by introducing two new ideas, viz. (i) the Minimum Subsistence Level (MSL) which denotes the minimum financial requirements of a household if its members are to 'maintain health and conform with Western standards of decency, i.e. be fully dressed and clean',[40] and (ii) the Humane Standard of Living (HSL) which attempts to determine a modest, low-level (but not subsistence) standard of living. The MSL and HSL for Durban Africans for May 1973 were calculated at R69,87 and R91,02 respectively,[41] whilst our mean PDL in June 1973 was R97,67.[42] Thus the MSL is only 70 per cent of our mean PDL, which is itself a subsistence measure, and even the HSL, which includes items such as medical care, education, recreation, etc., is below our PDL. These new concepts should not, however, be confused with measures of poverty.

Clothing is usually the most difficult item to assess objectively.[43] In some studies the principle of income elasticity of demand has been used to determine the clothing poverty line, i.e. the point at which the number of additional units purchased decreases.[44] But in practice the clothing component is based on regional factors, e.g. climate, and is computed according to some socially determined standard.

Rein states that there is no accurate measure in respect of items such as fuel and housing, both of which vary according to regions and social customs.[45] But in computing the African PDL in Durban, housing costs in the townships are known, and fuel can be directly costed.

It is important to realize that the PDL cannot be calculated on a national basis. In a city such as Durban with a subtropical climate, clothing and fuel requirements are less than in the colder areas of the interior. There are also regional differences in food prices, while rent and transport costs vary from city to city.

There are two alternative methods of computing a subsistence level of poverty. The first is by the use of the Engel coefficient. This is based on the proportion of the household budget spent on food and, when multiplied by expenditure on food, provides an estimate of the total minimum budget required to keep a family out of poverty.[46] This method is used in Japan.[47] The second method, which is used in our PDL studies, is to cost separately each item necessary for subsistence.

Whichever method is used, the subsistence definition of poverty has been the subject of increasing criticism. Rein believes that it is 'arbitrary, circular and relative'.[48] It has also been argued that it involves a considerable amount of subjectiveness; each PDL calculation, for example, is based on its author's interpretation of the concept.[49] However, not all these criticisms apply to our method, which relates to a particular community in a particular locality at a particular time. The estimate of clothing durability is admittedly arbitrary. It is true that there is no medical consensus as to the nutritional table, but it is nevertheless based on scientific research and provides the best available data. For the remaining components our method of direct costing avoids circularity and subjectiveness. Thus our PDL components and costs are in part scientific (food), in part social (clothing), and in part defined (rent and transport).

There are additional difficulties over and above the dietary problem discussed earlier when it comes to computing a PDL in a multiracial country. Bettison points out that the PDL is inadequate in that it assumes that a household is a unit of consumption with no economic obligations beyond it.[50] This assumption is of only limited applicability in Western society but is much less so in African societies with their wide kinship system.

The use of wages as the sole source of income in some poverty studies has its shortcomings. In addition to wages many employees receive hidden benefits, e.g. free accommodation, free rations, subsidized food at work, free rail fares, clothing allowance, etc. Then too, as Townsend points out, there are different 'degrees of combination between land/tribal and urban/industrial ties'.[51] In the Durban townships many people still maintain close ties with their rural areas. However, these are mainly migrant workers (who remit some 20–25 per cent of their earnings to the 'homelands') rather than household heads. Our PDL study is concerned with households, not with migrants; the qualification for family accommodation is 10–15 years' residence.

A further point pertains to housing. According to Schorr urban housing that falls short of specified standards can, through its influence on attitudes and behaviour, make and keep a family poor.[52] Housing will appear as slum housing if it falls too far short of the standard most people enjoy and countries can make their populations poor if they cut their housing investments too deeply. But this argument seems more applicable to a developed country, and in the light of our discussion on informal housing in chapter 5, there are difficulties in applying it in a semi-developed country such as South Africa where there is a wide disparity between the standard of housing enjoyed by Whites and that found in African townships. Yet the new township housing compares favourably with that of mass-housing schemes in the less-developed and 'intermediate range' countries. In South African cities there are in fact two completely different housing standards—one of Europe and one of Africa.

Most PDL and budget studies in South Africa have been conducted by White researchers. The danger here is that of a cultural bias on the part of the investigator. A good example relates to the Johannesburg African community in 1971[53] During that year the Johannesburg Chamber of Commerce estimated a family budget at R75,80 per month while the municipal non-European Affairs Department established a minimum budget (equivalent to the PDL) for a family of five of R69,86. Yet the Soweto Urban Bantu Council calculated the minimum budget of a family of five at R116,38; their food item was over R20 greater than that of the other bodies, and they included items such as tobacco and crèche fees and allowed significantly more for medical expenses, education and transport. Thus the poor themselves have a different conception of minimum needs than outsiders. Our study team has, however, always been multiracial, and cultural bias has thus been minimized.

There has been increasing criticism of the subsistence concept of poverty which dates back to Booth and Rowntree. Societies have changed during the twentieth century and so have human needs. Townsend writes: 'The subsistence concept seemed too static, somehow locked up in the distant youth of the grandparental generation.'[54] The concept of the PDL has remained virtually static since its introduction over 30 years ago, and this is one reason why the emphasis should perhaps be on the EML rather than the PDL as an indication of poverty.

But if we are to jettison the subsistence concept of poverty, what are we to substitute in its place? As alternatives to subsistence, Rein stated that poverty could also be conceived as inequality or externality. According to him the former 'is concerned with the relative position of income groups to each other' and the latter with 'the social consequences of poverty for the rest of society rather than in terms of the needs of the poor'.[55]

Townsend stresses the maldistribution of resources—poverty to him is a 'general form of relative deprivation'[56] stemming from such maldistribution. He mentions inequalities in the distribution of income, capital assets, occupational fringe benefits, and current public and private services. 'Poverty is not just a lack of resources required to live a normal live. It is a lack of resources in fact used, and felt to be rightly used, by the rich.'[57]

Thus poverty can also be seen as a concept embracing the lifestyle of the poor.[58] But problems arise once poverty is seen as a cultural and social as well as an economic condition. These problems are twofold, viz. first, where to establish the boundary separating the poor from the non-poor, and second, which non-economic conditions to take into account.[59]

Such issues may not be so simple when applied to South Africa. If poverty is viewed in the context of social stratification, it becomes an issue of inequality. It has been said that it is not pauperism but inequality that is the main issue in *high-income industrial societies*.[60] Now, economists generally view income inequality as an important factor in measuring development. Despite being regarded as a developed country by the United Nations, South Africa is in fact no more than semi-developed, displaying many characteristics of a less-developed country. In its dual economy is found both pauperism (in the form of abject poverty) and a highly skewed income distribution between Whites and Blacks.

New methods of estimating poverty are still being investigated. Some of these methods require more and better data than are currently available, e.g. on income distribution. Hubbard believes that the PDL is still a useful concept in South Africa because of the low standard of

living of the majority representing a state of physical and social deprivation, the general lack of other data, and the comparative lack of ex-
pense involved in fieldwork.[61] Whilst these three factors make the PDL
a convenient measure to adopt, there is a danger of overlooking the
investigation of new concepts by an over-reliance on the PDL. We
must guard against the danger of allowing our thinking to become
ossified.

We have already attempted to show that a separate consumer price
index for Africans is long overdue. Until such an index is constructed,
however, an annual revision of the PDL (such as we have done each
year since 1971) would provide a reasonable indicator of wage requirements. We have, in fact, compiled a mean PDL index[62] which, since
March 1973, has been revised on a quarterly basis. The base is March
1971, the date of the first of our recent series of PDL studies.

The PDL index and the CPI are not comparable. The former is a
simple unweighted arithmetic index the intention of which is to por-
tray changes in mean PDL costs. The CPI, on the other hand, is a
weighted index of expenditure. Whereas the PDL index covers only
subsistence costs of living, the CPI includes expenditure on all items.
The PDL index is therefore more restricted in range.

It is particularly important to note that whereas the CPI assigns a
weight of only 24,7 to food this item accounted for 73,5 per cent of
total mean PDL costs in 1973. Food prices have increased more rapidly
than those of other items, the CPI for food having risen from 104,1 in
April 1971 to 129,2 in April 1973. During the period April 1972–
April 1973 the CPI rose by 10 per cent compared with a 17,2 per cent
increase in the CPI for food. This is further illustrated in Table 6.9,
which shows that the PDL index for food increased more sharply than
that of all other items with the exception of taxation. The increase of
37,3 per cent in the food index between 1972 and 1973 is greater than
that of the CPI for food of 17,2 per cent mentioned above, and is due
to the fact that the PDL food items are concentrated in a narrow range

Table 6.9

MEAN PDL INDEX, MARCH 1972 AND 1973 (MARCH 1971 = 100)

Component	1972	1973
Food	114,5	157,2
Clothing	100,1	109,0
Cleansing	102,0	106,8
Fuel and lighting	109,0	113,2
Accommodation	100,0	100,0
Transport	100,0	112,1
Taxation	134,3	183,6
PDL	110,0	140,4

in which there are no effective substitutes and for which prices increased significantly, particularly in the second half of the period. It is thus not surprising that the PDL index shows an average annual rate of increase of 18,5 per cent between 1971 and 1973, which is much higher than in the case of the CPI which increased from 105,2 in April 1971 to 122,3 in April 1973, i.e. at an average annual rate of 7,8 per cent.

Since taxation is based on the PDL, the more rapidly the PDL increases the more rapidly will the taxation component increase. This is illustrated in the table.

Thus far the stress has been on costs rather than on income. But income could also be used as a yardstick by which to measure poverty, and in this connection an Australian study suggests that the poverty line should be adjusted each year in step with the index of average earnings.[63]

A concept which is being developed in Britain and which seems to hold out some promise is that of the *'deprivation index'*. Poverty may be defined in terms of relative deprivation which occurs when families or individuals are 'unable to have the types of diets, participate in the activities and have the living conditions and amenities which are customary in that society'.[64] Indicators are based on a list of activities and customs enjoyed by the majority of the population. In Britain these include, *inter alia*, summer holidays away from home, birthday parties for children and evenings out. Similar indicators can be selected for each country and a deprivation index can be obtained which will measure the prevalence of poverty.

The compilation of a deprivation index is easier in a homogeneous society than in a society consisting of different ethnic groups. But in any modern city the various ethnic groups are interrelated in the economic, institutional, legal, transportation, cultural and other systems. Despite racial segregation in, for example, the public transportation, educational, social and political systems, all race groups in South African cities share a common economic system and urban environment, and therefore adapt to certain social conventions and styles of life with many similar needs. But a particular group may nevertheless retain a degree of cultural self-containment— its activities and beliefs may remain relatively autonomous and its resources may differ from other groups. To that extent, therefore, it would be difficult to apply a national deprivation index to such a group.

Inequality of income and resource distribution in South Africa will be discussed in the following section; it is important that these factors be considered in a discussion of relative deprivation. But for the immediate purpose of compiling a deprivation index we need to define a style of living. This is done by distinguishing the types of customs and social activities practised or approved by a majority of the national population as well as a majority of the people in a locality, community or racial group, and the specific context and manner of expression of these customs or practices.[65]

A deprivation index can be applied to an urban African community in two respects: first, in relation to traditional social customs which the urban dwellers endeavour to maintain, and second, to new customs which are created in an urban environment.

There are a number of traditional Zulu ceremonies and obligations which the inability of a family to observe is considered a mark of deprivation, even in an urban community.[66] The following occasions, for example, require the slaughtering of an ox or goat and the supplying of food and beer: the wedding obligation ('*eyesikhumbe*'—literally 'ox of the skin'), funeral obligations on the death of an adult, the feast on the occasion of the termination of mourning, and the '*imbeleko*' ('first sacrifice') during the year following the birth of a child. In the case of '*lobolo*' ('bride price') cash has tended to replace cattle in the townships but it is not uncommon to find a *lobolo* consisting of both cash and cattle. In addition gifts are exchanged at a wedding. On the birth of a child traditional medicines have to be purchased; such medicines are also meant to fortify the home and this should be done at least every three years. In the case of certain illnesses traditional medicine is purchased in addition to that prescribed by a trained physician, so that medical expenses are often duplicated. Finally, it is customary to entertain friends at home and to offer them beer at least twice a month.

The joint cost of the *eyesikhumbe* and *lobolo* would amount to R200. The cost of the *imbeleko* and funeral obligations would approximate R20 each, and that of the death feast R40. Traditional fortifying medicines would cost R20 every three years, and traditional medical treatment R20 per year, while traditional home entertainment would cost at least R3 per month (using the cheapest beer).

Among the urban customs which might be included in a deprivation index are attendance at football matches, other sporting activities and *ngoma* dances; church contributions (especially for women); the purchase of a newspaper (either the twice-weekly Zulu or one of the English newspapers); and visiting the beach in summer (particularly among younger persons). Men endeavour to pay regular visits to *shebeens* which fulfil the role of a men's social club; township houses are considered too small for entertaining visitors. Among the younger age-groups the possession of a record player or radio is regarded as important in providing entertainment.

In summary, therefore, the PDL is intended to be a subsistence measure of poverty in a community; the extent of poverty is determined by relating the income of each household in a sample survey to its PDL (which is calculated separately for each household). The PDL has certain shortcomings, and to propose jettisoning it may appear paradoxical in a society in which wages all to often fail to reach that level. It is clear, however, that the distinction between 'primary' and 'secondary' poverty no longer serves any useful purpose, and the calculation of a Primary PDL is a meaningless exercise (except perhaps in small towns and 'company towns') since rent, transport and taxation payments are obligatory.

However, the PDL does perform several useful functions. In any country the calculation of some type of poverty line is useful in ascertaining the extent of poverty.[67] The PDL serves as the basis for calculating the EML which is a more realistic yardstick from which to gauge the extent of poverty and the wage requirements of a community. We have shown that, as long as income is below the EML, households economize on food in order to meet other requirements, and this is itself a mark of deprivation. But even the EML may not take sufficient account of social customs and it is suggested that it should be used in conjunction with measures such as the deprivation index if the extent of poverty is to be more accurately estimated.

During the last year, and particularly since the Black workers' strikes in Natal in the first quarter of 1973, the concept of the PDL has received much publicity. 'PDL' has become a catch-phrase in the press, both in South Africa and overseas, among those concerned with the White/Black income gap and foreign investment in South Africa, and has been put forward as the basis for a minimum wage. The term has been carelessly used and this has resulted in a widespread misunderstanding as to its significance. A clear distinction should be made between the proper use of the PDL as a measure of poverty and its misapplied use as the basis for a minimum wage. Whether the minimum wage can be set at a poverty line would depend on the circumstances of the particular country; it may, for instance, lead to the substitution of capital for labour and hence to greater unemployment and inequality, but its effects can be determined only by a detailed investigation. We have never advocated that the PDL be used as a basis for wages, and the fact that it is so used is because the PDL has been calculated in isolation without relating it to household income. Nevertheless, if the publicity given to the PDL has had the effect of increasing Black wages and making employers more aware of poverty, it will have served a useful purpose. In any country where wages are generally low, it is natural to look first at a PDL as a desirable minimum level for wages, but as wages increase the EML is clearly the more desirable level at which to aim. A danger exists, however, that society may attempt to salve its conscience by merely raising wages to a PDL level whilst ignoring the root causes of poverty and income maldistribution; should that happen the PDL would have diverted attention from the real problem.

AFRICAN POVERTY AND INCOME INEQUALITY

In this section the poverty of the African community is discussed in the broader context of inequality in the distribution of income in South Africa.[68]

EXTENT OF INCOME INEQUALITY

A wide gap has always existed in the earnings of the various race groups in South Africa. For example, the *per capita* incomes for the various groups in 1960 were calculated as follows: Whites R952, Asians R147, Coloureds R109 and Africans R87.[69] And a calculation for 1970 showed that Whites received an annual *per capita* income of R1 939 compared with R150 for the Black groups combined; the figure for the population as a whole was R461.[70] In many instances the White/African wage gap has widened in the last few years, despite the fact that the government and the private sector have frequently mentioned the social and political dangers inherent in the existence of this disparity.

Thus, in private manufacturing industry the White/African earnings ratio rose from 5,1:1 in May 1966 to 5,9:1 in July 1972; in the gold-mining industry during the same period the ratio increased from 17,5:1 to 21,0:1.[71] In the building and construction industry the ratio increased from 5,8:1 in March 1967 to 6,1:1 in May 1972. Small changes, mainly unfavourable, in the White/African salary and wage ratio in commerce and finance occurred between 1969 and 1972. The ratio rose in banking from 3,9:1 to 4,1:1, in the wholesale trade from 5,1:1 to 5,5:1, and in retailing from 3,4:1 to 3,5:1, while a decrease from 4,6:1 to 4,2:1 was recorded in insurance. In the public sector, between March 1969 and the second quarter of 1972 the ratio increased from 6,2:1 to 7,1:1 in provincial government and from 6,1:1 to 6,3:1 in local government, while in central government it decreased from 6,0:1 to 5,5:1. Between 1968 and 1971 the ratio in the railways rose from 5,4:1 to 6,0:1. However, growing wage inequality has been masked by the increases in African real incomes noted earlier in this chapter.

CAUSES OF INCOME INEQUALITY

The reasons for the existence of the income gap are to be found in the institutional structure of the South African labour market. The main features of this structure are:

(1) The White group, by virtue of its political power, has acquired a virtual monopoly of skills. Competition from Blacks is prevented by legislation, hence there is an artificial shortage of skilled labour (which is becoming more critical each year) and wages for skilled labour are bid ever higher.

(2) As a corollary to (1), there are a host of legislative restrictions on the acquisition of skills by Blacks and on the movement of African workers to the urban areas. Thus it has been stated that 'as in no other capitalist society, the producers here are reduced solely to their role in production—elements in an exchange process, cheap raw material in the calculation of costs'.[72] This results in a large pool of labour engaged in subsistence or near-subsistence agriculture in the 'homelands', which provides an elastic supply of unskilled labour in the modern sector.

The seminal work on income distribution in South Africa is that of Knight.[73] He claims that the White labour force has monopolized skilled employment through job reservation legislation, influx control, trade union policy and the operation of the educational and social (and, it may be added, the political) system. All these devices cannot stop the absorption of Blacks into more skilled jobs during periods of economic expansion, but they do operate 'to preserve the White monopoly of skills in periods of recession'.[74] Thus White and Black labour may be treated as separate factors of production. His analysis shows that the White wage rate may be regarded in two ways, viz. either as a reflection of the higher productivity at the margin of White relative to Black labour or as monopoly rent accruing to a factor in highly inelastic supply.[75]

However, not all Whites are skilled and not all Blacks are unskilled. But even in the areas of overlap Whites and Blacks receive unequal pay for equal work, e.g. teachers, clerks, mechanics, etc. According to Knight the reasons for the higher wages of unskilled Whites are the 'socially determined factor-mix (i.e. the overseer must be White) and the high wages available to such workers in alternative employment'.[76] One reason for the high transfer earnings are the wage and employment practices in the public sector which offers sheltered employment to unskilled Whites who would otherwise have to compete on the un-skilled labour market at Black wage rates. Conversely, the lower wages of skilled Black workers are explained by their lower transfer earnings and the failure to substitute Black for White labour through social pressure and restrictions on racial competition. 'Since the forces of substitution are not permitted to operate, the White wage rate is nothing but an artificially-created scarcity rent.'[77]

The income gap cannot, however, be measured only by considering relative wage rates. White labour saves a proportion of its income, and profits derived from accumulated savings increase the size of the gap since Black workers find it difficult to save.

According to Van der Merwe the most important determinant of conditions on the African labour market is the labour bureau system with its attendant regulations and administrative procedures.[78] The Bantu Labour Act of 1965 provided for the establishment of labour bureaux, of which there were 130 in the Zulu 'homelands' in 1968. These labour bureaux operate mainly at two levels, viz. local and district. He refers to the 'very complicated institutional framework within which the forces of Bantu supply and demand have to operate in South Africa, as compared to those economic systems upon which the standard textbooks on the labour market are based'.[79]

Labour bureaux were created in order to correlate the supply of and demand for African labour. Both the local (mainly urban) and district (mainly tribal) bureaux are faced with an inelastic market demand for African labour.[80] In contrast, the supply of African labour is elastic;

this is particularly true in the case of district labour bureaux in the 'homelands' where supply greatly exceeds the number of employment opportunities.

Thus the labour bureau system has led to the disintegration of the African market, creating a separate labour market in the area of jurisdiction of each bureau. Moreover, it has created different competitive conditions on the different labour markets with regard to the number of workseekers and employers. There are relatively more workseekers on district bureaux markets and relatively more employers on local bureaux markets.

CONSEQUENCES OF INCOME INEQUALITY

The consequences of the income gap are that South Africa has one of the most highly skewed income distributions of all countries. Archer refers to the 'remarkable paucity of information' on income distribution in South Africa.[81] Various studies have allocated 70–76 per cent of total income to Whites;[82] Archer then calculates that the wealthiest 10 per cent of the population (assumed to be all White) receives some 58 per cent of total income.[83] 'There are few countries indeed which . . . have a more skewed distribution; and probably no other which has this skewness coupled with the advanced structural characteristics of the economic system found in South Africa.'[84] Archer stresses the tentative nature of size distribution measurements and international comparisons, but concludes that '. . . the South African income structure exhibits such a gross skewness that, even after making allowance for error and exaggeration, we are faced still with a unique degree of inequality within one economy'.[85]

The figure of 58 per cent above may be compared with estimates for the United States of 27–28 per cent, Pakistan and Japan 30 per cent, Denmark and Britain 31 per cent, Taiwan 26 per cent, Argentina and Ceylon 37 per cent, Mexico 41 per cent, Colombia and Brazil 42 per cent, Philippines 40 per cent, Senegal 48 per cent, Madagascar 50 per cent and Gabon 60 per cent.[86]

In South Africa the ratio (White) skilled wages to (Black) unskilled wages is 8:1 compared with the ratio of 1,4:1 in the United States (the ratio among South African Whites is also 1,4:1).[87] Steenkamp points to the fact that the average wage differential between unskilled and skilled wages in Europe varied between 20 and 30 per cent of the former whereas in South Africa the figure was 400–600 per cent.[88] But, as Kessel points out, it is more pertinent to ascertain whether the skilled/unskilled wage differential in South Africa is greater than that in countries at similar levels of development.[89] He states that cursory examinations indicate that the real earnings of White workers in South Africa are considerably higher than those in Britain and Italy and marginally higher than in Australia.

It is anomalous that in a country at an intermediate level of development one small section of the population should be enjoying one of the highest standards of living in the world while the majority are living in poverty. The artificial scarcity of skilled (White) labour has forced employers to bid ever higher for workers and has led to extremely rapid wage and salary increases as well as the promotion of Whites to managerial positions 'for which they are unqualified and which they could not have occupied under normal market conditions'.[90] It is not surprising that such management is frequently criticized for being inefficient and ignorant of the needs and circumstances of the Black labour force.

REDUCING INEQUALITY

The question of Black wages and narrowing the income gap is one of the major current topics of debate in South Africa—among academics, politicians and businessmen and in the press.[91] During the early 1960s Black wages were the subject of several articles in the *South African Journal of Economics*. Thereafter the debate slackened off somewhat only to be resumed with greater force in 1970.

Much of the debate was centred on the role of the Wage Board. Pursell found that from 1957–8 to 1962–3 the Wage Board was an important influence in increasing real earnings of Africans, but that from 1963–4 employers voluntarily raised real earnings above the minimum rates.[92] Pursell's thesis is challenged by Spandau, who believes that market forces have had a greater impact on wage differentials than is generally realized.[93] According to Pursell the primary objective of the Wage Board has been to increase African real earnings, and he sees Wage Board differentials as reflecting the will of the government while real earnings differentials reflect the play of free market forces. But as Spandau points out, Wage Board policy constitutes only a small portion of South Africa's labour policy and has had only a limited influence on prevailing wage structures.[94] The average racial wage gap in fact widened during the 1960s, both in absolute and relative terms. Between 1959–60 and 1970, average monthly wage rates for Whites in mining increased by 90 per cent compared with only 47 per cent for Africans; in manufacturing the figures were 94 per cent and 82 per cent and in construction 106 per cent and 86 per cent.[95] These figures led Spandau to conclude that had the government been serious about improving African earnings relative to Whites it would have tackled the mining sector first. However, the Wage Board has never investigated the mining sector; its failure 'to redress this most notable occurrence of inequality is further evidence of the lack of a general "new deal" for Bantu'.[96]

Two other factors which have received a great deal of attention in the income-gap debate are inflation and productivity. The articles by Hume and Kessel are particularly pertinent in this respect.[97]

Hume argues that it is White wage movements which have been

inflationary in the sense that they have exceeded the growth in productivity. In contrast, African wage movements have usually failed to reach the productivity growth line and have never exceeded it. Kessel states that Hume has underestimated the likely impact on prices of increasing Black wages by 10–20 per cent per year for five years; taking all Black groups into account he believes that costs and prices could rise by 2,1 per cent per annum compared with Hume's 0,75 per cent.[98] An important factor, for which there is no evidence on which to base predictions, is the reaction of White workers to substantial increases in Black wages which would narrow the skilled/unskilled wage differential. Thus the argument turns full circle to the redistribution of income in South Africa.

Two important items in the redistribution of income are White incomes and business profits. Kessel writes that if substantial wage increases to Blacks are not to be unduly inflationary, White workers and White owners of capital 'will have to be willing to accept a slower (if not zero or negative) rate of growth in their incomes'.[99]

We have already shown that skilled, i.e. White, wages in South Africa are artificially high because of protective legislation. The result is that in many occupations wages are higher than the job is worth. Etheredge, for example, places truck-driving in this category.[100] He feels, therefore, that the introduction of the 'rate for the job' is not the solution as it would merely mean paying Blacks the artificially high wages which have developed. For some jobs the existing White wages are not inflated and similar rates should be paid to Blacks. But in those jobs with artificially high wages, a 'unified wage scale' should be introduced on the basis of the realistic market price for the job. His detailed description of the operation of such a scheme is based on the Copperbelt in the days of the now defunct Federation of Rhodesia and Nyasaland.

Some of Etheredge's proposals might be open to criticism, but the important point is that if all restrictions on Black labour were removed South Africa would still be no more than a medium-income country and a considerable amount of poverty would remain. Increased competition for skilled jobs would slow down (and perhaps even halt) the increase in skilled incomes, and whilst it would obviously be unrealistic to expect White incumbents of certain jobs to take wage cuts, a new 'unified wage scale' would lead to the reduction of wages in many jobs today reserved for Whites. Blacks doing similar jobs would find their wages rising to the new level and thus the position of Black semi-skilled and skilled workers would improve and the wage gap would be narrowed. But in the case of unskilled workers the removal of labour bureaux would merely increase the flow of migrants to the urban areas; the elastic supply of unskilled workers would ensure that wages for this group would remain at a very low level as is the case in less-developed countries.

Minimum wage legislation might tend to reduce unskilled employment through factor substitution. There is clearly a trade-off between raising wages and providing more employment opportunities. Kessel refers to the likelihood of reduced demand for, and hence unemployment of, unskilled Black labour 'much of which is not absolutely essential to the production process'.[101] Included in this category are domestic servants, chauffeurs, messengers, tea-makers, etc. But he believes that higher Black wages are not necessarily incompatible with increased employment opportunities in skilled and semi-skilled occupations. Economic growth (which would be facilitated by an expanding domestic market as a result of increased Black incomes) would create more jobs than those destroyed by wage increases; this is particularly true of skilled and semi-skilled labour, which is seen as the key to growth.

Knight believes that an imposed increase in the Black money wage will 'tend to reduce unskilled employment in the modern sector through factor substitution. This in turn will impoverish further the traditional sector.'[102]

But the narrowing of the income gap cannot be tackled on only one front. Prescribed minimum wages or the formation of Black trade unions alone are not enough. Knight lists three additional measures which would be required to raise the real market wages of Black labour:[103]

(i) The development of African agriculture in order to increase marginal productivity in the 'homelands' and hence the wage rate at which workers are willing to enter the modern sector.

(ii) The gradual exclusion of foreign unskilled labour (from neighbouring countries) which increases the elasticity of supply of unskilled labour and delays the rise in unskilled rates.

(iii) The most important measure is the 'destruction of the economic colour bar by means of social, educational and legislative reform, with consequent collapse of the present dichotomy between unskilled Black and skilled White . . . .'.

Although wage differentials account in large measure for the income gap, there are other factors which sustain and widen the gap. The ownership of wealth in the form of assets, e.g. land, stocks and shares, savings and investments, is overwhelmingly in the hands of Whites, and income received from these assets must also be considered. Fringe benefits received from employers usually accrue to persons in top positions and substantially improve the living standards of such persons. The distribution of public social services such as health, education and social security is also an important factor in income inequality, while a qualitative factor is the distribution of resources such as public utilities (electricity and water), recreation facilities, education and health services, etc. Income inequality, and hence deprivation among Blacks, is perpetuated by the whole web of discriminatory legislation preventing the acquisition of skills, the undertaking of certain jobs, labour mobility, etc., as well as discrimination at all levels of government in the provision of public services. The inferior facilities provided in the African townships of Durban are clearly illustrated in chapter 5. There are many systems—economic, social and political—which distribute resources and benefits to individuals, families, groups and communities, and the reduction of inequality in South Africa would require structural change in several institutional systems.

CONCLUSION

Poverty in South Africa is a reflection not only of wide cultural differences but also of inequality in the power structure. The existing social and political system has led to a highly skewed income distribution pattern with extremes of affluence and poverty at either end of the spectrum. The abolition of restrictions on labour utilization and an increase in the vertical mobility of labour would lead to the reduction of extreme affluence and to a more equitable distribution of income among skilled and semi-skilled workers. But in the short-term, because of the elastic supply, it would not have a significant effect on the great mass of unskilled workers. Large-scale poverty would remain, in both rural and urban areas, but extreme inequalities, which are the danger point in any society, would be reduced.

NOTES AND REFERENCES

1 G. R. Feldmann-Laschin & H. Saks, *Income and Expenditure Patterns of Urban Bantu Households—Durban Survey*, Pretoria: University of South Africa Bureau of Market Research, Research Report No. 13, 1966, and Nel *et al.*, op. cit., henceforth referred to as BMR Report 1964–5 and BMR Report 1970–1 respectively.

2 The consumer price index adjustment has been computed on the basis of increases in the official consumer price index of 9,1 per cent between 1959 and 1964 and 21 per cent between 1964 and 1970. These proportions have been applied to the increase in African household costs between 1959 and 1970 of 59,1 per cent. The calculation gives an increase in the index for Africans of 16 per cent for the first period and 37,2 per cent for the second period.

3 BMR Report 1964–5, op. cit., Table XXV.

4 Ibid., op. cit., Table XXXIX.

5 Ibid.

6 In the 1959 study the median income from other sources of 20 cents is 3 per cent of the median wage income.

7 BMR Report 1964–5, op. cit., Tables XXVI and XXXVI.

8 Described in chapter 5.

9 The assumption here is that the proportion of women in domestic service is maintained.

10 BMR Report 1970–1, op. cit., p. 1.

11 Ibid., p. 3.

12 Michael Hubbard, *African Poverty in Cape Town*, Johannesburg: South African Institute of Race Relations, 1972, p. 50.

13 Heribert Adam, *Modernizing Racial Domination: The Dynamics of South African Politics*, Berkeley: University of California Press, 1971, p. 97.

14 BMR Report 1970–1, op. cit., adapted from Table 3.7(a). In this calculation the 84 adult children workers have been added to both total population and total earners.

15 Ibid.

16 The 84 adult children earners have been added to the total number of earners.

17 See BMR Report 1964–5, op. cit., Table XXX, and BMR Report 1970–1, op. cit., Table 1.1.

18 See BMR Report 1964–5, op. cit., Table XXX, and BMR Report 1970–1, op. cit., Table 3.9.

19 Ibid., based on 'Items Bought' in Table 3.20(a).

20 P. N. Pillay & P. A. Ellison, *The Indian Domestic Budget*, Durban: Natal Regional Survey, 1969, p. 72.

21 E. Batson, *The Poverty Datum Line in Salisbury*. School of Social Science and Social Administration, University of Cape Town, 1945, p. 14.

22 This section is based on: P. N. Pillay, *A Poverty Datum Line Study Among Africans in Durban*, Occasional Paper No. 3, Durban: Department of Economics, University of Natal, 1973.

23 The median-sized household was one of 5 persons. We have, however, used the mean in preference because of the weighting procedure employed.

24 The two-roomed houses at KwaMashu are not regarded as permanent accommodation: they are used as temporary transit accommodation for residents until four-roomed houses become available.

25 Though the 20 cent levy for education is not normally regarded as a PDL item, it is a compulsory monthly payment and is included in the assessment made here for rent.

26 Home-ownership schemes are excluded because of the difficulty of relating the monthly instalment and maintenance to a rental charge. The onus of maintenance in these schemes is on the occupier.

27 BMR Report 1970–1, op. cit., Tables 3.14(a), 3.10(a) and (b).

28 Ibid. Table 3.16(c).

29 This suggests a defect in the statement by Potgieter & Roger that 'the income difference between the Effective Minimum Level and the Secondary Poverty Datum Line may be accounted for by the earnings of other members of the household . . ., ranging from 1.4 to 1.8'. See: J. F. Potgieter & D. B. Roger, *The Poverty Datum Line in Port Elizabeth, Uitenhage and Despatch*, Institute for Planning Research, University of Port Elizabeth, 1972, pp. 23–4.

30 Margaret A. Young, op. cit., and H. L. Watts, *The Poverty Datum Line . . .*, op. cit.

31 This would of course apply likewise to total expenditure on PDL items.

32 See Peter Townsend (ed.), *The Concept of Poverty*, London: Heinemann, 1970, and especially the contributions by Townsend (chapters 1 and 5), Martin Rein (chapter 2), Brian Abel-Smith and Christopher Bagley (chapter 4), Alvin L. Schorr (chapter 6) and S. M. Miller and Pamela Roby (chapter 7); and also the discussion in the Rhodes–Livingstone Journal, *Human Problems in British Central Africa*, by: David G. Bettison, 'The Poverty Datum Line in Central Africa', no. 27, 1960, pp. 1–40, B. Thomson & G. Kay, 'A Note on the Poverty Datum Line in Northern Rhodesia', no. 30, 1961, pp. 39–49, and 'A Reply to the Note' by Bettison in the same issue, pp. 49–53.

33 Rein, op. cit.

34 Thomson & Kay, op. cit., p. 46.

35 P. A. Nel, M. Loubser & J. J. A. Steenekamp, *The Minimum Subsistence Level and the Minimum Humane Standard of Living of non-Whites living in the Main Urban Areas of the Republic of South Africa, May 1973*, Research Report No. 33. Pretoria: University of South Africa Bureau of Market Research, 1967.

36 J. F. Potgieter, *The Poverty Datum Line in the Major Urban Centres of the Republic*, Research Report No. 12, Institute for Planning Research, University of Port Elizabeth, 1973.

37 Unpublished study by H. L. Watts and H. J. Sibisi, Institute for Social Research, University of Natal.

38 Potgieter, op. cit., p. 60.

39 Pillay, op. cit., p. 13.

40 Nel *et al.*, op. cit., p. 1.

41 Ibid., p. 27.

42 Pillay, op. cit., p. 30.

43 Bettison, 'The Poverty . . .', op. cit., p. 12.

44 Rein, op. cit., p. 51.

45 Ibid.

46 Ibid., p. 50.

47 Abel-Smith & Bagley, op. cit., p. 95.

48 Rein, op. cit., p. 60.

49 Thomson & Kay, op. cit., p. 40.

50 Bettison, op. cit., p. 20.

51 Townsend, op. cit., p. 38.

52 Schorr, op. cit., p. 123.

53 Horrell, op. cit., 1971, p. 177.

54 Townsend, op cit., p. x.

55 Rein, op. cit., p. 46.

56 Townsend, op. cit., p. 2. Townsend develops this concept further in his contribution entitled 'Poverty as Relative Deprivation: Resources and Style of Living', in Dorothy Wedderburn (ed.), *Poverty, Inequality and Class Structure*, Cambridge University Press (forthcoming).

57 Ibid, p. 45.

58 Ronald F. Henderson, Alison Harcourt & R. J. A. Harper, *People in Poverty: A Melbourne Study*, Monograph No. 4, University of Melbourne Institute of Applied Economic and Social Research, Melbourne: Cheshire, 1970, p. 16.

59 Rein, op. cit., p. 47.

60 Miller & Roby, op. cit., p. 124.

61 Hubbard, op. cit., pp. 3–4.

62 Pillay, op. cit.

63 Henderson *et al.*, op. cit., p. 2.

64 Townsend, *The Concept* . . ., op. cit., p. 42.

65 Townsend, 'Poverty as . . .', op. cit.

66 We are indebted to Harriet Sibisi, Research Fellow in the Institute for Social Research, University of Natal, for providing us with this information.

67 This point is discussed by Dudley Seers, 'What are we Trying to Measure?', *Journal of Development Studies*, vol. 8 no. 3, April 1972, p. 28.

68 For a more detailed general discussion see: *Power, Privilege and Poverty*, Report of the Economics Commission of the Study Project on Christianity in Apartheid Society, Johannesburg: Spro-cas, 1972.

69 C. Bak, *Het Verbruik en de Destribute van Textielproducten in de Republiek van Zuid Afrika*, Unpublished D. Com. thesis, University of South Africa, 1964.

70 A calculation based on the 1970 population census by Ivar Ostby, Department of Economics, University of Natal.

71 The ratios mentioned in this paragraph are calculated from earnings figures contained in: Muriel Horrell, *A Survey of Race Relations in South Africa* (annual).

72 Adam, op. cit., p. 96.

73 J. B. Knight, 'A Theory of Income Distribution in South Africa', *Bulletin of the Oxford University Institute of Economics and Statistics*, Vol. 26 No. 4, November 1964, pp. 289–310.

74 Ibid., p. 294.

75 Ibid., p. 296.

76 Ibid., p. 297.

77 Ibid.

78 P. J. van der Merwe, 'The Economic Influence of the Bantu Labour Bureau System on the Bantu Labour Market', *South African Journal of Economics*, vol. 37 no. 1, March 1969, p. 42.

79 Ibid., p. 45.

80 Ibid.

81 Sean Archer, 'Inter-racial Income Distribution in South Africa: Data and Comments', Paper presented at a Seminar of the Abe Bailey Institute of Inter-racial Studies, University of Cape Town, November 1971, p. 2.

82 It is interesting to note that as far back as 1903–4, 69 per cent of GGP accrued to Whites. See Zbigniew A. Konczacki, *Public Finance and Economic Development of Natal* 1893–1910, Durham, N. C.: Duke University Press, 1967, p. 198.

83 Archer, op. cit., p. 8.

84 Ibid.

85 Ibid., p. 9.

86 Ibid.

87 D. A. Etheredge, 'Wages, Productivity and Opportunity', Paper presented to the Annual Conference of the South African Institute of Race Relations, Johannesburg, January 1973, pp. 4–6.

88 W. F. J. Steenkamp, 'Bantu Wages in South Africa', *South African Journal of Economics*, vol. 30 no. 2, June 1962, p. 100.

89 Dudley Kessel, 'Non-White Wage Increases and Inflation in South Africa', *South African Journal of Economics*, vol. 40 no. 4, December 1972, p. 372.

90 Spro-cas Report, op. cit., p. 30.

91 In January 1973 the University of Natal's Department of Economics launched a three-year study project into various aspects of closing the income gap.

92 Donald E. Pursell, 'Bantu Real Wages and Employment Opportunities', *South African Journal of Economics*, vol. 36 no. 2, June 1968, p. 94.

93 Arnt Spandau, 'South African Wage Board Policy: an Alternative Interpretation', *South African Journal of Economics*, vol. 40 no. 4, December 1972, p. 384.

94 Ibid., p. 383.

95 Ibid., p. 386.

96 Ibid., p. 385.

97 Ian Hume, 'Notes on South African Wage Movements', *South African Journal of Economics*, vol. 38 no. 3, September 1970, pp. 240–56, and Kessel, op. cit., pp. 361–76.

98 Kessel, op. cit., p. 366.

99 Ibid., p. 368.

100 Etheredge, op. cit., p. 7.

101 Kessel, op. cit., p. 374.

102 Knight, op. cit., p. 307.

103 Ibid., p. 308.

CHAPTER 7

Towards KwaZulu

This study was focused primarily on poverty and housing in an urban setting. Both are intimately connected with rural–urban migration and rural poverty, which is an important cause of such movements. We conclude the study, therefore, by examining the implications for an urban community of incorporation in the 'homeland' of KwaZulu, and the potential role of the townships in the development of KwaZulu. But first a brief description of KwaZulu itself.

KWAZULU

KwaZulu was born out of the system of African Reserves which was established in Natal in the middle of the nineteenth century.[1] With the advent to power of the National Party government in 1948 the Reserves in South Africa gradually took on a new significance; in terms of the proclaimed goal of separate development the African people, who are subordinates in the existing political system, may change their status through self-determination in a system of nine politically independent states (Bantustans or 'homelands').[2] However, the Bantustan policy merely 'deflects political aspirations to areas where they are no danger to White rule'[3] whilst retaining the economic links between the White areas and the new satellites.

At present KwaZulu consists of 29 separate pieces of land scattered throughout Natal. However, in 1972 the government announced its proposals for consolidating KwaZulu into five separate large blocks together with a small block near the proposed port of Richards Bay. This was followed by final consolidation proposals in 1973 which provide for ten separate blocks (Map 6), the future of two of which is still being considered.

Best and Young point out that throughout history states have desired political and spatial cohesion. 'The ideal or model nation-state is one in which there is political stability, economic progress and social improvement, and where the *raison d'être* is both supported and strengthened. A single spatial unit is more favourable to the realisation of these conditions than a fragmented state, especially one interspersed with alien territory and a contradicting *raison d'être*.'[4]

Government proposals for 'homeland' consolidation in KwaZulu have been severely criticized by academics and by politicians of all races in Natal.[5] Not only will the process take many years to complete in the face of opposition from Whites and Africans alike, but without territorial contiguity the administration of a modern state becomes

135

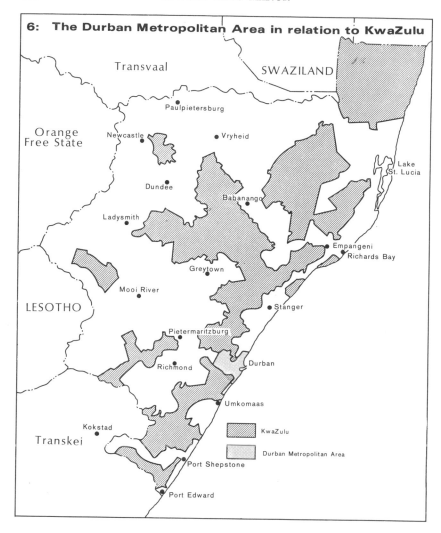

6: The Durban Metropolitan Area in relation to KwaZulu

Transvaal

SWAZILAND

Orange
Free State

Paulpietersburg

Newcastle   Vryheid

Lake
St. Lucia

Dundee

Babanango

Ladysmith

Empangeni
Richards Bay

Greytown

Mooi River

LESOTHO

Stanger

Pietermaritzburg

Richmond   Durban

Umkomaas

KwaZulu

Kokstad

Durban Metropolitan Area

Transkei

Port Shepstone

Port Edward

extremely difficult. It has been pointed out that apart from human resources other factors also assist in promoting the economic, social and political well-being of a country; these are '. . . a consolidated territorial base, a territory that is not excessively misshapen, a section of coastline with a natural harbour, a wide natural resource base, a favourable man-land ratio, and strategically located growth points and transport routes'.[6]

The proposed consolidation plan for KwaZulu falls down on all these points. Apart from the magnitude of administrative problems posed, no major economic resource or centre of development in Natal is included in KwaZulu. Both the existing and proposed ports and all major urban centres, which provide employment opportunities for the Zulu people, remain in White Natal. as do the coalfields, the

most productive agricultural areas, viz. the sugar belt and the Natal
Midlands, and three of the four game reserves which would provide a
base for the tourist industry. The exclusion of Richards Bay, which
is to be developed into a large metropolitan area and heavy industrial
centre, has been particularly criticized. A feature of Map 6 is the reten-
tion of White corridors to the coast, notably those to Durban and
Richards Bay.

Because the national boundaries of KwaZulu have still to be finalized
in detail, and the administrative framework is new, statistical data are
either non-existent or at best grossly inadequate. But estimates have
put the Gross Domestic Product at R45,9 million in 1967–8 and the
per capita income at R109,1 in 1966–7.[7] It seems certain, however, that
barring unforeseen mineral discoveries KwaZulu as it is presently
envisaged will be independent in name only.[8] The economic problems
faced by most small countries would be compounded in the case of
KwaZulu by the lack of spatial cohesion, and it would be 'a captive
economy of South Africa, dependent on that country for the employment of a large proportion of its labour force and for grants-in-aid
to balance its budget'.[9]

The government's consolidation proposals in fact represent nothing
more than a slight modification of the boundaries of the existing
Reserves. Nevertheless they entail large population movements which
are a feature of the implementation of the policy of separate development. Some 133 000 Africans would have to be resettled from the
excised Reserve areas, which would become White, and 17 000
persons of other races would have to leave KwaZulu. In addition there
are some 400 000 Africans in White rural areas of Natal who are being
resettled in KwaZulu, usually in special camps on a site-and-service
basis. Although some of the latter group are able to commute to their
previous places of employment, these movements can only add to
population pressure in KwaZulu.

The amount of land available to Africans in South Africa has been in
virtually fixed supply, while population has increased rapidly. The
result is that in the 'homelands' population pressure, and hence agriculture, resemble conditions in Asia rather than elsewhere in Africa where
land tends to be more plentiful[10]. The declining land–man ratio and
increasing incidence of soil erosion in KwaZulu have been remarked
upon by official commissions since the 1930s, and indeed were major
causes of the rural–urban population drift which gathered pace at
that time.

Agricultural conditions in KwaZulu vary; some areas were under-
stocked as recently as 1965, but more commonly there is widespread
overstocking and soil erosion, and low crop yields are obtained. For
example, the average maize yield in KwaZulu is 262 kilograms per
hectare compared with the 2 262 kilograms per hectare obtained by
White farmers in the Transvaal Highveld.[11] Maize is the staple crop

in the 'homelands'. Similarly, yields of other crops such as sorghum and wheat are also low. These crops are produced mainly by subsistence farmers.

The Tomlinson Commission recommended that one-half of the families on the land in the Reserves be removed in order to reorganize African agriculture.[12] This report has been criticized by Lipton on the ground that, given the shortage of land and plentiful supply of labour, labour-intensive agriculture (with peasants on small irrigated and arable plots) rather than capital-intensive should have been adopted.[13] This would reduce the number of families who would be required to leave the land. Moreover, it is argued that the Commission failed to make sufficient allowance for agricultural labourers on large holdings, thereby further overestimating the number of peasants required to be moved from the land.[14]

In the event the land-reform scheme proposed by the Tomlinson Commission has proved too ambitious to attempt. But if Lipton is correct the 'homelands' could accommodate many more people on the land than previously envisaged. In many parts of KwaZulu, however, it is doubtful whether a labour-intensive scheme could be successfully applied until a soil rehabilitation programme has been undertaken, and this would be a lengthy task.

Lipton recognizes that the 'homelands' will remain dependent on the White areas for employment opportunities.[15] Although the successful adoption of a labour-intensive agricultural policy and a rural development programme would reduce the rate of rural-urban migration, the formulation of a dynamic urbanization policy would be an important factor in providing productive employment for the growing labour force. It is therefore to the townships of the DMA that we now turn.

IMPLICATIONS FOR THE TOWNSHIPS

Of the existing African townships in the DMA only Umlazi is situated in KwaZulu. However, KwaMashu is to be incorporated in 1975, and with the advent of the Bantu Administration Area Boards the path is opened for the incorporation of Umlazi Glebe. It is much easier in Natal than in the other provinces to incorporate the African townships in the major cities into the 'homelands', thereby implementing the goals of separate development with regard to the geographical separation of the race groups and the 'return' of Africans to the 'homelands' (in Natal the 'homelands' abut metropolitan areas so that boundaries can be easily changed; this is not the case in the rest of the country). It is reported that Lamont and Chesterville, both of which now fall under such boards, will ultimately cease to exist as African areas. Lamont adjoins Chatsworth and would be developed as an Indian area, while Chesterville exists as an isolated African area in the midst of White suburbia. Thus the hapless Africans will lose their two oldest and best established townships, and the only Africans residing in the Durban city limits would be domestic servants and others housed on private and licensed premises and in government compounds.

The Durban African population is at present part, albeit a disadvantaged and underprivileged part, of a semi-developed economy. But should the National Party government proceed with its policy of separate development to the point where KwaZulu becomes independent, the Durban Africans will be part of a country which would qualify for classification as 'least developed'.[16] This would have certain implications for the role of the townships in economic development.

Although much of the literature on economic development neglects the role of the city as a decisive agent in the transformation of societies, and instead tends to stress the social problems of cities, urbanization has been closely linked by some writers with economic growth. Friedmann, for example, believes that urbanization is an important development tool and advocates a strategy of deliberate urbanization in less-developed countries.[17] A useful analysis is that of Hoselitz who states that a city can be either 'generative' or 'parasitic' in its effect on economic development in surrounding regions.[18] It is generative if its impact on economic growth is favourable, i.e. if its formation and continued existence and growth are a factor accounting for the economic development of the region; it is parasitic if it exerts the opposite effect.

An examination of the relationship between Durban and its surrounding regions reveals a duality. Whether a city is generative or parasitic is closely related to the character of the economic system—its productive capacity, transportation network, technology and income levels. The economic structure of the regions surrounding Durban is dual in character, consisting of a modern and a subsistence sector. The dual economy also has a spatial dimension, the modern sector being roughly coterminous with the developed White and Indian-occupied areas and the subsistence sector with the 'homelands'.

Has Durban then been generative or parasitic? In its relationship with the developed areas the city has generated demand stimuli which have had favourable effects on agricultural production, industrial output and employment. In contrast, however, the only linkage which has been established with the 'homelands' is that for labour. Urban growth has failed to trigger off any response in the way of increased agricultural or industrial output in the 'homelands'; the traditional subsistence economy with production for own consumption has remained relatively unchanged over time in its relationship to external markets. Durban's functions have been orientated to the requirements of a modern technological society, and at the same time that urban growth has been taking place changing land–man ratios and declining productivity of the soil in the 'homelands' have resulted in the rural economy failing to meet the subsistence needs of the growing population.

On the supply side we need to consider two aspects, viz. (i) the positive effects of urban growth on creating a pool of skills that would otherwise not have been available, and (ii) the negative effects of urban growth on the productive capabilities of the traditional economy.[19]

The creation of a pool of skills could have efficiency stimulating effects on attitudes, habits, tastes and discipline. But in South Africa the existence of the migrant labour system with its high rate of labour turnover, and job reservation, has meant that the development of a substantial pool of skills among Africans has been frustrated. Moreover, those skills acquired in the cities cannot often be put into use in improving agricultural productivity in the 'homelands'.[20]

Furthermore, since the migrant labour system is highly selective (involving mainly able-bodied males) and since migrants are frequently the most active and enterprising individuals, the system results in a decline in agricultural productivity and a loss of economic and social leadership in the 'homelands'. In this sense the cities may be parasitic, retarding the growth of the 'homelands' economy.

The important question, however, is whether the migrants would have applied their energies to improving agricultural methods and output if the traditional economy had remained undisturbed. Is there any evidence, for example, to show that those Africans living closest to Durban have tended to produce for the market rather than accept wage employment? Another important point on which we have little information relates to the utilization of cash flows, i.e. remittances from migrants. Are these used to augment rural consumption (in which case they constitute leakages) or are they converted into capital improvements in agriculture? And are migrants, once having been wage-earners, more likely to produce for the market upon their return to the homelands? Available evidence, though scanty, suggests a fairly substantial leakage and a negative answer to the remaining questions.

It appears, therefore, that Durban's generative impact has been directed mainly to the modern sector and that its growth has contained parasitic elements as far as the 'homelands' are concerned. But the parasitic impact does not appear to have been particularly strong. Parasitic effects must be thought of in terms of the productive uses to which the resources claimed by the urban economy could have been put, and of the different pattern of economic growth and income distribution that might have emerged.

So much for the past relationships between Durban and the 'homelands'; what of the future? Cities are also points in the space economy and, if an economic system changes, whether cities are generative or parasitic in the new system is a function of their position in the new spatial integration that emerges.[21] The creation of an independent KwaZulu implies the creation of a new national economy and a new political and social system for its people. To what extent therefore can these new forces lead to KwaMashu and Umlazi becoming generative cities in their relationship to the rural areas of KwaZulu?

Because of the close economic interdependence that would remain between KwaZulu and the White areas, the urban centres of KwaZulu would clearly have to be discussed in relation to the overall southern African space economy. However, it seems that a new urban sub-system could emerge in KwaZulu and that KwaMashu and Umlazi could take on new functions. This might depend on the extent to which the scope for spatial change inherent in the creation of a new national economy is limited by fragmentation.

At present KwaMashu and Umlazi are merely dormitories supplying labour to the White areas. But the emergence of a politically inde-pendent KwaZulu could have important consequences for the economic and social life of the townships. They would have an opportunity to provide employment through industrial and commercial growth, and also to stimulate commercial agriculture by constituting a market for fresh vegetables, meat, eggs, dairy products, etc. KwaZulu's economic policy towards its cities could be framed with a dual objec-tive: (i) to reinforce rigorous measures for agricultural reform by generating a growing demand for foodstuffs and industrial raw materials, and (ii) creating urban conditions in which potential external economies could be utilized.

The urbanization policy in an independent KwaZulu would have important social and economic implications. At present influx control restricts the flow of Africans to the existing urban areas in South Africa; it has been used to buttress the migrant labour system and to discourage the families of workers from moving to the towns. A manifestation of this policy is the large hostels for single men in KwaMashu and Umlazi. The great majority of these men are migrants and are in fact married, their families having remained behind in the 'homelands'. The migrant labour system has for long been attacked on the grounds that it gives rise to social problems and the argument has been well catalogued by Wilson.[22] By lifting influx control the KwaZulu government could encourage families to join the breadwinners, thereby introducing a settled family life in the urban areas and overcoming the socially undesirable effects of the migrant labour system.

This would mean a large influx of people to the townships in the short term, implying an increase in the urban population of perhaps 50 per cent. This would impose a serious housing and urban infrastruc-ture burden on the KwaZulu government. The hostels would become redundant as such but could perhaps be converted into apartments, while 'site-and-service' schemes could be permitted. In addition to the advantages of such a policy (discussed in chapter 4), it would prevent scarce funds having to be diverted to mass housing. The majority of those who would migrate to the urban areas would be wives and children who would not be economically active but would demand urban services and education facilities, so that substantial investments would, however, have to be made in less-productive social sectors.[23]

The effect of such population movements on the rural sector would be to alleviate population pressure and facilitate steps to improve agriculture. It could be particularly important to promote family migration to urban areas in order to offset the influx to KwaZulu of the 400 000 persons who, as noted above, are being moved from White rural areas.[24]

It should be stressed, however, that such family migration merely means that *existing* urban dwellers will be joined by their families. As in most less-developed countries so too in KwaZulu will it be important to reduce the rate at which *new* migrants flow to the urban areas. It has been mentioned above that the reduction of this flow will depend to some extent upon policies in the rural areas. But it will also depend upon narrowing the real income differential between urban and rural areas. The KwaZulu government would, therefore, have to adopt a wage-restraint policy in the urban areas, although the existence of higher wages in the adjoining White areas would continue to attract migrants to towns such as Umlazi and KwaMashu.[25]

A further consequence of independence would be the possibility of the KwaZulu government encouraging the creation of central business districts and the development of industry in the townships.[26] At present Durban's African townships are merely residential areas and from an economic point of view are satellites of the central city. The few small businesses which have been established have a low turnover, and the shops and markets of the central city continue to attract township residents. Moreover, the residents rely on the central city for services such as banking, insurance, etc.

As part of the DMA it would be difficult for KwaMashu and Umlazi to meet the competition from the central city; in any metropolitan region the central city tends to maintain its commercial dominance. KwaMashu and Umlazi would be the largest cities in KwaZulu, and although in terms of central place theory and the rank–size rule[27] it is unusual for the two largest cities of a country to be of approximately equal size, they would, if developed, act as the service centres for different spatially separated areas of KwaZulu.

It would appear sound strategy for KwaZulu to develop these two townships as part of an incipient urban hierarchy. Thus an attempt could be made to create a central business district (CBD) in each of the two townships by encouraging the establishment of African-owned businesses and services and of branches of South African firms, e.g. chain-stores, insurance companies, building societies, etc. There is considerable resistance from White entrepreneurs towards the granting of trading and manufacturing licences in the townships because of the fear of losing a lucrative African market. Lipton quotes the example of East London's African township, Mdantsane, where only two licences for bakers have been granted and East London bakeries continue to supply bread.[28] An independent KwaZulu government would have no difficulty in controlling such a situation.

In this way the townships would become towns in the true sense of the word. The firms would be registered in KwaZulu and thus a corporate tax base would be created, while additional local employment opportunities would be created, thereby widening the personal tax base; this is important in less-developed countries which characteristically have weak personal tax bases. The presence of a local 'downtown' area, together with passport and currency control on residents crossing the border to shop in Durban, would encourage commuters employed in Durban to spend their earnings in KwaZulu, and leakages would therefore be reduced to a minimum.

In addition to the development of CBDs, the KwaZulu government would be provided with scope to attract industry to the townships. Both KwaMashu and Umlazi would be able to offer the agglomeration economies of the metropolitan region, and would appear to be more favourable locations for industry, in the short-term at any rate, than Isithebe (just north of the Tugela River) which is being developed as the industrial growth point for KwaZulu by the Bantu Investment Corporation.[29] Young has shown that land suitable for industry can be found close to both townships.[30] A small industrial area has already been demarcated in Umlazi, and the KwaZulu government could give more attention to the servicing of industrial land. Rail spurs would have to be constructed, but the townships are no further from the Durban harbour than the successful industrial estates of Pinetown, New Germany and Prospecton, and are reasonably well placed in relation to railway routes along the coast and to the interior. The development of industry in KwaZulu would be important in providing employment as well as export earnings and corporate tax revenue.

The commercial and industrial development of KwaMashu and Umlazi would not, however, reduce their dependence, at least in the short term, on the Durban central business district for a wide range of expertise—legal, financial, commercial banking, insurance, import–export, advertising, technical and distributive.

The replacement of the migrant labour system by a normal settled family life, and the commercial and industrial development of the townships, may be construed as advantages for the residents. But it should be pointed out that neither of these two advantages is one that could not be had at far less cost in a shared multiracial South African society. Moreover, these advantages would apply only to townships in those metropolitan areas which straddle 'homeland' boundaries. In this respect the African community of Durban (and also of Pietermaritzburg) is better placed than most others; these advantages would not apply to isolated townships in White areas such as Soweto near Johannesburg and Langa in the Western Cape. There

freehold rights do not apply, influx control operates and the population
is entirely commuter.

There are other implications, too, of incorporation into KwaZulu.
Firstly, it would perpetuate urban service differentials within the same
metropolitan region. Thompson has discussed the problem of inter-
municipal income inequality within metropolitan areas in the United
States, as a result of which the less affluent local authorities provide a
lower standard of services and public goods.[31] In the DMA, because of
the large inter-racial income disparities, the African local authorities
would be financially incapable of providing comparable facilities,
both in quality and range, to those in the adjoining White towns.
In the past the White areas have always received preferential treatment
in the provision of paved streets, storm-water drainage, street lighting,
etc. To this extent the position so far as the townships are concerned
would be no different; as we have seen they are self-financing. But
there has always been the hope, and indeed the expectation, that in the
long term the townships would share the common Durban municipal
budget. Now, residential segregation has become formalized by
political fragmentation, and the differentials will be perpetuated.

Secondly, the fact that the DMA would transcend national boundaries
poses the problem of controlling international labour movements.
A large number of commuters from the townships would be crossing
international boundaries twice each day on their way to and from
work. No doubt some agreement could be entered into between the
two countries to obviate passport control in the case of commuters,
which would be a tedious and perhaps impossible operation. But as
discussed above it would be advantageous for KwaZulu to control
casual shoppers from crossing the border.

CONCLUSION

The fifteen-year period covered by this study has seen the evolution
of the political doctrine of separate development from almost total
White 'baasskap' (domination) to the proposed territorial partition of
South Africa. For the African community of Durban it has been marked
by a massive rehousing programme. The former shack dwellers now
live in improved physical conditions, and poverty does not appear as
acute. Real incomes have increased, and indeed there is visible evidence
that many Africans are materially better off than fifteen years ago.
But the incidence of poverty is still great, both in the DMA and in the
rural areas, as is illustrated by the continued rural–urban drift of population and the emergence of new shack settlements. And relative to
Whites incomes have not improved.

Although incorporation into KwaZulu will mean an improvement of
family life, the freedom from pass laws and police raids, the opportunity
to own a house, and participation in local (and national) government,
these benefits could be secured by alternative policies.

Through the years the African community has played an important part in the development of the modern industrial economy of the DMA. In the normal course of events any disadvantaged group would hope that it would ultimately share the fruits of a common economy and society. Instead, political fragmentation is seen as perpetuating inequality and relegating the African community to becoming citizens of a less-developed country.

NOTES AND REFERENCES

1 For a historical description see Edgar H. Brookes & N. Hurwitz, *The Native Reserves of Natal*, Natal Regional Survey Vol. 7, Cape Town: Oxford University Press, 1957, and also Muriel Horrell, *The African Reserves of South Africa*, Johannesburg: South African Institute of Race Relations, 1969.

2 Adam, op. cit., p. 2.

3 Ibid., p. 69.

4 Alan C. G. Best & Bruce S. Young, 'Homeland Consolidation: The Case of KwaZulu', *South African Geographer*, vol. 4 no. 1, September 1972, p. 62.

5 See ibid., and Gavin Maasdorp, 'Targets of Development in Relation to Population Trends and Needs', Paper presented at a conference on Comprehensive Development in Zululand, Institute for Social Research, University of Natal, Durban, February 1972.

6 Best & Young, op. cit., p. 68.

7 J. Adendorff, 'Problems in the Creation of Infrastructure and Techniques Applied in the Development of Zululand', Paper presented at a conference on Comprehensive Development in Zululand, Institute for Social Research, University of Natal, Durban, February 1972.

8 For a recent appraisal of the Bantustan policy see Merle Lipton, 'Independent Bantustans?', *International Affairs*, vol. 48 no. 1, January 1972, pp. 1–19.

9 Maasdorp, op. cit., p. 18.

10 Merle Lipton, 'The South African Census and the Bantustan Policy', *The World Today*, vol. 28 no. 6, June 1972, p. 264.

11 Horrell, *A Survey . . .*, 1972, p. 190.

12 Union of South Africa, *Summary of the Report of the Commission for the Socio-economic Development of the Bantu Areas within the Union of South Africa*, UG 61/1955, Government Printer, Pretoria.

13 Lipton, op. cit., p. 264.

14 Ibid., p. 265.

15 Ibid., p. 266.

16 One criterion for such classification is that manufacturing accounts for less than 10 per cent of GNP; see Percy Selwyn, 'The Least Developed Countries at Santiago', *Bulletin*, Institute of Development Studies at the University of Sussex, vol. 5 no. 1., January 1973, p. 21. In the Zulu areas of Natal the figure is only 4,4 per cent; see Adendorff, op. cit.

17 John Friedmann, 'The Strategy of Deliberate Urbanization', *Journal of the American Institute of Planners*, vol. 34 no. 6, November 1968, p. 364.

18 Bert F. Hoselitz. 'Generative and Parasitic Cities', *Economic Development and Cultural Change*, vol. 3 no. 3, April 1955, p. 279.

19 Barber, op cit., p. 114.

20 Absalom Vilakazi, *Zulu Transformations*, Pietermaritzburg: University of Natal Press, 1962.

21 Mabogunje, op. cit., p. 22.

22 Wilson, op. cit., chapter 9.

23 Blair, op. cit., gives a thoughtful discussion of an urban planning and housing policy for African cities.

24 So far as KwaZulu is concerned, this would appear to answer Friedmann's query (op. cit., p. 366) as to whether his strategy of deliberate urbanization would be applicable in Africa.

25 If South Africa were to remain in its present form, a policy of narrowing the White–Black income gap would be more important than reducing African migration to the cities. In an independent KwaZulu, however, the reduction of rural–urban migration rates and rural–urban real income differentials would be of high priority in development strategy. The existing chain of migration in Natal may be thought of as follows: rural sector→ urban informal sector→ urban wage sector (although the links can be bypassed). The introduction of an international boundary adds a further link in the chain: rural sector→ urban informal sector in KwaZulu→ urban wage sector in KwaZulu→ urban wage sector in Natal. The position in KwaZulu would be much the same as in, for example, Lesotho, where the opportunity cost of unskilled male labour is related to the wage structure in the (White) South African cities. Thus, if KwaZulu adopted an urban wage restraint policy, higher paid jobs in the White cities would be highly sought after by its citizens.

26 See Maasdorp, op. cit., p. 10 and Bruce S. Young, 'The Industrial Geography of the Durban Region', Unpublished Ph.D. thesis, University of Natal, 1972, pp. 385–9.

27 For a summary of these concepts see Richardson, op. cit., chapter 7.

28 Lipton, op. cit., p. 267.

29 Maasdorp, op. cit., p. 10. See also Adendorff, op. cit., for a brief discussion of the locational disadvantages of Isithebe.

30 Young, op. cit.

31 Wilbur R. Thompson, *A Preface to Urban Economics*, Baltimore: Johns Hopkins University Press, 1964, chapter 3.

Index